🔲🔲🔲🔲🔲

THE HOUSE OF HANOVER

🔲🔲🔲🔲🔲

THE MIRROR OF BRITAIN SERIES

General Editor : Kevin Crossley-Holland

THE HOUSE OF HANOVER

🐚🐚🐚🐚🐚🐚

ENGLAND IN THE 18th CENTURY

🐚🐚🐚🐚🐚🐚

Leon Garfield

ANDRE DEUTSCH

First published 1976 by
André Deutsch Limited
105 Great Russell Street London WC1

Copyright © 1976 by Leon Garfield
All rights reserved

Printed Offset Litho in Great Britain by
Cox & Wyman Ltd
London Fakenham and Reading

ISBN 0 233 96636 6

'The proper study of mankind is man.'
POPE. *Essay on Man.*

꙰꙰꙰꙰꙰

ACKNOWLEDGEMENTS

꙰꙰꙰꙰꙰

Acknowledgements are due to the following for permission to reproduce the colour and black and white plates: The Trustees of the British Museum, 32a, 32b, 32c, 32d; Building, Newspaper for the Design and Construction Team, 28; A. F. Kersting, 14; The National Portrait Gallery, *1, 2, 3, 4, 5, 6, 7, 8, 9, 10, 11, 12, 13, 14, 15,* 1, 2, 3, 4, 5, 6a, 6b, 7, 8, 9, 10, 11, 12, 13, 15, 16, 17, 18, 19, 20, 21, 22, 23, 24, 25, 26, 27, 29, 30, 31, 33, 34, 35, 36, 37, 38, 39, 40, 41, 42, 43, 45, 46, 47, 48, 49, 50; Radio Times Hulton Picture Library, 44a, 44b.

꧁꧁꧁꧁꧁

CONTENTS

꧁꧁꧁꧁꧁

To Pam Royds

᪺᪺᪺᪺᪺᪺

INTRODUCTION

᪺᪺᪺᪺᪺᪺

THINK of this as an appetizer – a seasoning, if you will – to a rich dish of history: a turbulent, crowded hundred years, or so, when three Georges, one after another, sat on the throne of England and steadily lost their German accents; while round about them two great political parties connived and jockeyed for power. The Tories – adherents to the lost cause of banished King James II – were out; the Whigs – welcomers of William of Orange – were in. Whigs and Tories. Queer names; both, as befitted politics, were terms of abuse. Whigs from a poor man's drink – a sort of milk that had gone off; and Tories from Irish outlaws of the most savage and incoherent type.

It was an age of Empire building, of Indian adventures and crazy South Sea finance; a quarrelsome, greedy time; a time of foreign wars and domestic upheaval; a time of hectic rushes for money, driving the countryfolk into the towns, to turn them into warrens of filth and poverty which forever crowded upon the stately mansions of the newly rich.

London was the middle of this almost civilized world; and here is London in the midst of the century, its qualities listed by Gwynn, in the year 1750:

1 Ordure left lying in the streets, and especially at the posterns of the City gates and on the north of the Royal Exchange.
2 Rubbish lying in heaps in the streets.
3 Open cellar doors or stone steps projecting into the street.
4 Broken pavements.

5 Ruinous houses.
6 Sheds for shops placed against the walls of churches.
7 Streets blocked up with sheds and stalls.
8 The encroachment of newly built houses into the street.
9 The driving of bullocks through the streets.
10 The prevalence of mad dogs.
11 The swarms of beggars.
12 The deluge of profanity in the streets.
13 The absence of lighting in the streets . . .

In the House of Lords, a peer complained that: 'The present neglect of cleansing and paving the streets is such as ought not to be borne; the passenger is everywhere either surprised and endangered by unexpected charms, or offended and obstructed by mountains of filth . . .'

Yet out of such a dunghill, what has been called the Augustan age was born. A fastidious age, an age of fine proportion and elegant craftsmanship and high distinction in letters. An age of some virtue, too – of great philanthropists, religious reformers and staunch upholders of human rights; an age that produced in abundance men whom many a cleaner age might well have envied. But then great cleanliness and great goodness have not always gone together: the two most celebrated examples of washing – Pontius Pilate and Lady Macbeth – are not renowned for their virtue.

In a slender appetizer, much of this cannot be touched upon. The great furniture makers – the Chippendales, the Sheratons, the Hepplewhites; the china factories of Wedgwood, Chelsea, Derby and Bow, and the host of unnamed builders who made the squares, terraces and villas of the Georgian towns must give way to the more urgent claims of those ink- and paint-stained gentlemen who walked the streets and whose thought still colours our own. Besides, the craftsmen are a melancholy subject whose story belongs more with the Industrial Revolution that eclipsed them and changed the meaning of 'manufacture' from 'made by hand' to 'made by machine'. The craftsmanship of the age was a brief marvellous flowering that has quite vanished save in the longing of human beings for some sort of making of things in which they may still take a pride. A great deal has been talked and shouted about the dignity of labour; most of all nowadays when labour itself has been stripped of all joy and dignity, and a man's spirit is driven to rebellion and strike, not against wages and conditions, but against the tedious humiliation of serving a machine.

Leave them, then, the craftsmen; it is our deepest tragedy that they are dead.

It's true that Henry Fielding Esquire, of Bow Street, may have sat in a chair made by Chippendale, drunk from a Chelsea china cup, told the time by one of Tompion's clocks and warmed himself before a fireplace shaped by Robert Adam. But the cups and clocks are museum-bound now; it is only Henry Fielding himself who can still be in our house and mind.

If, in the wayward course of what follows, one reader is persuaded to Henry Fielding, or Jonathan Swift, or Hogarth, Defoe or Handel, then the chief aim of this appetizer will have been realized, and the journey will not have been in vain. Time travellers – embark.

᭤᭤᭤᭤᭤᭤

OF all the doorways into the past – whether through books, learned histories, dusty museums or the broadcast sagas of lecherous kings and their whining queens, there's none that harnesses the imagination so aptly as the glass and mahogany revolving door of the National Portrait Gallery, just off Trafalgar Square.

Pick a rainy day; there's nothing like rain in London for provoking a longing to be anywhere else in space and time. Penetrate the gallery's shadowy recesses, rich with the smell of wood and furniture polish; mount the stairs, or if the rain looks like going on for ever, wait for the lift. At all events, obey the gallery's injunction to 'begin at the beginning'; I speak from experience . . .

'Where is the House of Hanover?' I asked the attendant as I handed in my dripping umbrella for safe keeping.

'Just after the House of Orange, sir.'

'Is that upstairs?'

'If you begin with the Plantagenets . . .'

'Then I'll be all day at it.'

'The rain looks to be set in for a long while, sir.'

'But I've only come in to look at Handel and Hogarth – and Richardson and Pope, for that matter . . .'

'And very agreeable, too, sir. I often go and look at Mr Handel myself. A fine face. A gentleman of some humour and strength, I fancy. Pardon me for asking, but are you musical, sir?'

'Only as a listener.'

'Like myself, sir. I'm very fond of a little Handel, now and then.'

'Which room is he in?'

'If you begin at the beginning, you can't miss him, sir.'

'Is it really necessary?'

'If you'll excuse the liberty, sir, you won't do him justice, else.'

'How do you mean?'

'There's his wig, his clothes, his sword . . . he'll look so quaint to you, coming in straight from the street. You will be looking at him, so to speak, over your shoulder. He'll be someone you've passed by. I don't mean to offend, sir, but you won't be able to help being condescending and patronizing. And I'm sure you don't mean to patronize the composer of *Saul* and *Messiah*.'

'God forbid!'

'If I might put it this way, sir – and I speak from deep familiarity with all the ladies and gentlemen on our walls – if you was to go direct to your destination, you would fancy that you'd stepped among waxworks – tableaux in fancy dress. I used to find it so myself, sir, when I began here . . . and I often wondered if the past was real and what it all had to do with me. Have you ever been to Australia, sir? By air I mean?'

I shook my head, much confused.

'You go from winter to summer in a day, sir. And you ask yourself where has the spring gone? It's as if time has been pulled out of joint and a season you can't quite believe in has been painted over the crack. If you know what I mean.'

'You're quite a philosopher.'

'When the occasion arises, sir. I attend evening classes.'

I stared at him, but not the ghost of a smile flickered over his face.

'So there is no way to the House of Hanover except from the beginning of the street?'

'Happy image, sir, if I may say so. Are you literary?'

He looked down; and added modestly: 'We have a great many literary gentlemen in the House of Hanover.' At the same time he handed me what for a moment I took to be a medal but turned out to be the numbered disc that identified my umbrella. Unaccountably blushing, I thanked him and hurried away towards the lift. I pressed the button; a light came on above the closed doors indicating that the lift was in the basement. It did not seem to be working.

'It's in one of its moods, sir. Unfortunately we are not mechanically minded here.'

The basement light went out; the lift was moving – it remained to be seen in which direction.

'If I might make so bold, sir –'

'I'll start at the beginning; I promise.'

'If I might give you a *tip*, sir –'

I felt in my pockets when the attendant, who had floated to my side and was watching the closed doors of the lift with melancholy expectation, put up his hand and shook his head rather wistfully I thought.

'I was not hinting, sir. The age of patronage has passed us by. I meant only to inform.'

I blushed again and wondered what could have become of the lift.

'The tip I had in mind was that as you walk from countenance to countenance on our walls, you refrain from looking at the names. Look at the faces, sir, and make up your own mind whether it's a saint or a sinner in the frame. Mistakes have been made. I don't mean to imply we are ever negligent and lay the wrong name under the right face, as you might say; but sometimes, when the names are fastened on the wall – there being no room on the frame – there can be confusion about where they belong: above, below, or sideways. You wouldn't credit it, sir, but we have had visitors seeing shuddering cruelty in the face of John Locke (a thinker, sir, and gentle), and the milk of human kindness running out of the eyes of Judge Jeffreys on account of the labelling being indecisive. However, we've sorted that one out. There's no mistaking the judge; now, that is.'

The lift arrived; the doors opened and I stepped inside.

'Second –' began the attendant; but before he had time to say 'floor', the doors had closed and I was alone, travelling imperceptibly towards the House of Plantagenet.

After five hundred years, give or take a few, the lift stopped. I smiled, and then, unwillingly intrigued by the talkative attendant's notion, I resolved to consult the portraits' faces before reading the names.

I remember drifting into fantasy and imagining the heavy frames lengthening and dissolving into doorways through which the painted multitude would step and discourse on statecraft and the affairs of olden times, giving me many sly little bits of news the years had covered over. I stepped from the lift and, briefly closing my eyes, tried to smell the stuff of their robes and the sacred oil that had anointed their heads. I opened my eyes and was confronted by – a charade, a wretched pretence of face after yellowing face, staring meaninglessly out of darkness. There was some Russian Christ, said to be King Richard II (see plate 1); there was the profile of a wooden saint, said to be King Henry V (see plate 2). Then another Richard, an Edward or so, a pair of

1. Richard II   2. Henry V

3. Henry VIII

Henrys and sundry tight-lipped dames who may or may not have
been their queens.

They were not portraits, but icons, the dim religious labours of anonymous journeymen whose distance from their high subjects was no less great than their distance from God. No sky appeared, no servants to be seen in the awful blackness; for all one knew, ghosts or mice tended the sunless faces and brushed the iron robes. Did they ever live, I wondered?

I drifted on among the Tudors; ghastly faced, with poison in their eyes (see plate 3). Power, arrogance and brutish cruelty marked all but a tragic few (see plates 4 and 5) . . . and on them, the fear of sudden death (see plates 6a and 6b) . . .

4. Thomas Cranmer   5. Jane Seymour

But little by little I became aware that the anonymous journeyman of old had taken upon himself the right to look his monarch in the eye – and not like what he saw. But still he laboured with circumspection; 'Artist Unknown'.

Then, suddenly, the Court of Queen Elizabeth explodes. A great door seems to have opened, or a wall been broken down; a gaudy host of new men have burst in to strike improbable attitudes round the walls (see plates 7, 8 and 9), rivalling in their splendour the tinsel grandeur of the smiling Queen herself (see

6a. Anne Boleyn

6b. Katharine Parr

colour plate 1). Here and there a painter signs his name; and it is a great step.

In the midst of this flashy concourse appears an abrupt and almost frightening centre of gravity, like some life's head at a feast of death. Heavy eyed and impenetrable, Shakespeare stares out, reminding the onlooker of immortality; the creator of history whose Richards and Henrys forever stalk the mind and dissolve into well-graced actors who say no more than he has set down for them (see colour plate 2).

Hypnotized, I stared at him and became full of vague thoughts concerning illusion and reality, thoughts stirred by half-remembered speeches from 'Hamlet' and 'The Tempest' . . . until I was impatiently pushed aside by other dreamers on the prowl.

I departed and went through an archway to where the well-mannered Stuarts held court in a gallery where the lighting was improved. King James I sat, or, rather, slumped in his throne, brooding on the evils of tobacco and gunpowder, and longing, above all, for literary eminence (see plate 10). Around him are

7. Sir Philip Sidney

8. Robert Dudley, Earl of Essex   9. Sir Walter Raleigh

10. James I

11. Ben Jonson   12. John Donne

13. Inigo Jones

14. The Queen's House, Greenwich. The north front.

those who achieved it; sturdy Ben Jonson (see plate 11), rival to Shakespeare and so learned that he probably farted in Greek (they were a coarse lot, the Jacobeans); and there's John Donne, looking more the conspirator than the poet (see plate 12). Next to Donne gazes a man who, were he not clearly labelled, might well have been taken for a poet in a mood of inspiration (see plate 13). Here is a man amazed by wonders; a poet in stone – an architect. Painted by Sir Anthony Vandyke, Inigo Jones seems to have been caught in that very moment of delighted admiration when he first saw the villas of the architect Palladio in Italy and resolved to carry back the Italian's designs to enrich his native England. It was Inigo Jones who designed the lovely 'Queen's House' in Greenwich (see plate 14), for the wife of Charles I.

Charles I himself, the last of the divine kings, stands hard by. Small of stature, ineffably gentle, his aspect is more sad than arrogant; it is as if he feels the world does not quite see him as he knows himself to be. Beside him rests his jewelled crown that looks as if it would have cracked him like an egg. Gazing at this painting, one cannot but feel that it was needless to have cut off that pathetic head to reduce the monarch's stature; the artist had done it more surely and more compassionately with his brush – some eighteen years in advance of the axe (see plate 15).

Somewhat dreamily I left this king and observed with pleasure that the rise of the artist – and with him, the generality of men – continued apace. Vision widens and a sense of human inquiry creeps in at every door. Charles II, best of kings, is obliging enough to exhibit in his magnificent face every conceivable human frailty excepting the vicious (see colour plate 3). In the space of two hundred years in time and a dozen yards in space, I had come a star-distance from the carved Plantagenets. I looked about me. Samuel Pepys, a commoner, stared back as proudly as any Tudor noble; he held in his hand not a sword, but a scrap of music (see plate 16). John Bunyan, a tinker's son, one-time dancer on the village green and gaol-bird, smiled at me with more than royal confidence. And well he might, for he holds that unique masterpiece, *The Pilgrim's Progress*, which was the

15. Charles I

16. Samuel Pepys

first great work of English prose to have reached the common people (see plate 17).

As one century runs into the next and the Stuarts fade into the House of Orange, the quantity of 'Misters' represented increases even as the Earls and Dukes decline. I caught sight of

John Locke, the great philosopher, looking wonderfully knowing and strangely humorous for one of his solemn calling. He it was, in his *Essay Concerning Human Understanding*, began modern criticism of all knowledge. He it was also, who, less grandly, first

17. John Bunyan

put the idea into parents' heads that children should be happy while they learn (see plate 18).

Beside him is Henry Purcell, the greatest native-born English composer. He died before the century changed, at the age of thirty-six. According to rumour (not hard to believe when one studies his face), the tragedy was a consequence of having been locked out by his wife after coming home drunk with his friends and singing rude songs of his own composing in the street outside the lady's window. He caught cold, it seemed . . .

18. John Locke   19. Henry Purcell

He left behind him – and in front of him, too, for he was a forward-looking man – a vast treasury of beautiful songs and a way with the setting of English words that has never been surpassed. Listen to 'I attempt from love's sickness to fly' and marvel how the music soars and dips on the word 'fly', depicting precisely both the yearning and the striving for physical flight (see plate 19).

One J. Closterman painted him, and Greenhill painted John Locke. Gone for ever are the days of 'Artist Unknown'. Now the painters' names figure equally with the sitters, sometimes even eclipsing them. Sir Godfrey Kneller lays about him with a facile brush, grandly declaring his fee to be 'twenty guineas with one hand showing'.

Although Sir Godfrey studied in the school of Rembrandt, was admired by the Duke of Monmouth and Charles II, he was not quite a great painter. However, what is almost as important, he was considered one, so great men were content to sit for him.

Look: there's a Kneller, in the grand manner. A gentleman in flowing garments and a loose cravat. A darkly waved wig, a quizzical look, at once sensual and aristocratic. Only the fact that one hand is showing marks the sitter as a twenty guinea man and not some haughty peer well able to afford both hands and feet into the bargain. Who is he, then, who gazes with such humorous contempt towards the House of Hanover? Something about the face suggests that here is a man Sir Godfrey respected, perhaps even feared. Look closely; this is John Dryden, poet and satirist. His pen was so devastating that once he was waylaid and almost killed by men hired by a statesman he'd held to public scorn (see plate 20).

Near by, on an adjacent wall, hangs another Kneller, but not in the grand manner. Here is a disagreeable face; a painting with not even one hand showing; a painting with an oddly unfinished look – as if the artist and sitter had been unable to bear each other's company for another moment. A man with a broad brow, a heavy jowl, morose but penetrating eyes and a stretched mouth. A lawyer? A judge? Not strict enough in his dress. His cravat is untied – as if he'd been disturbed in dressing. Plainly he could not be bothered with the niceties of social life.

Like John Dryden, he gazes towards the next age, but not with amusement. He does not seem to care for what he sees, even though he is responsible for much of it. Discovering an underlying order in the Universe, Sir Isaac Newton shook the foundations of faith and turned God into a master of Arithmetic. Small wonder he looks so grim; even his skull, one feels, is frowning. According to those who knew him and talked with him, he was a humble, modest man and many of his preserved

20. John Dryden

sayings are calculated to foster that impression; according to Sir Godfrey Kneller, who stared at him for hour after hour and reproduced what he saw with his own sharp eyes, he was cold, impatient of courtesy, and poor company (see plate 21).

In old age, Sir Isaac declared that his most famous discovery –

the Law of Gravity – came to him from watching an apple fall. Apples have never been mankind's luckiest fruit; but at least Sir Isaac waited for his apple to fall; unlike Eve, he did not steal it from the tree.

With what relief the painter turns to Sir Christopher Wren! Fine velvet coat, superb cravat, and both hands extravagantly

21. Sir Isaac Newton

painted . . . in one of which is a pair of dividers against the plan of a church. Sir Christopher smiles; and well he might: Surveyor General of the Royal Buildings, eminent in Geometry, Astronomy and Architecture. Already his head looks like the dome of St Paul's. Fifty-one churches to his almost eternal credit . . . also glass eyes and a model of the moon. Sir Isaac Newton thought highly of him, and something suggests that so did Sir Christopher Wren. And why not? He made beautiful things that have given much use and much pleasure (see colour plate 4).

Look – there's William Wycherley, to the very life! He might have been taken sitting by that open window of the tavern in Bow Street, opposite his home. He has, on his pleasant face, that look of half-hearted innocence of a man who does not know what to conceal from the eye of his watchful wife (see plate 22). Wycherley, the first great master of the English witty comedy, was, in a way, the victim of his own productions. Though he railed against hypocrisy and fawning flattery, he was not averse from using them when the occasion arose. He dedicated his masterpiece *The Plain Dealer* to the Duchess of Cleveland and at once became her lover. Thus he made the discovery that sour grapes may be palatable after all. His ambition thereafter turned from literature to life – and he aimed his sights at obtaining a rich and high-born wife. Romantically, he found one. He overheard a beautiful, unknown lady asking for a copy of *The Plain Dealer* in a bookshop. She turned out to be a wealthy widow and a countess to boot. 'Fy! madam, do you think me so ill-bred as to love a husband?' Wycherley had written in *Love in a Wood* – his first play. Unfortunately the lady turned out to be ill-bred and loved him most exclusively. She would not let him out of her sight for a moment; she allowed him only to drink with his friends in the tavern opposite their house . . . and then she demanded he sat by the window and kept it open so that she could be sure she was not sharing him, even with a barmaid. She died a year after their marriage, carried off, presumably, by a chill; but the ill-wind that brought it on was one that blew nobody any good. The playwright's reasonable expectations – for which he'd already given up the profitable favours of the Duchess of

1. Elizabeth I

2. Shakespeare

3. Charles II

4. Sir Christopher Wren

22. William Wycherley

Cleveland – were most unfairly shattered. His dead wife's family disputed her will and Wycherley spent a fortune fighting them in the courts. He lost – and then spent seven years in a debtor's gaol, being unable to meet the costs he had incurred. When he was seventy-five, he risked marrying again – this time a young girl. Perhaps, like King David, it was only for warmth; or perhaps

23. Sir John Vanbrugh

it really was, as unkind friends suspected, merely to prevent his
nephew inheriting his estate.

But the inheritance of his achievement was subject to no
restraint. A smallish part of this inheritance went to Sir John

Vanbrugh. See him there, painted, as usual, by Sir Godfrey
Kneller. A somewhat fleshy young man, with prematurely tired
eyes as if he'd never quite got over having to write in a bad light
(see plate 23). Like Wycherley, he went to France to study and
become a gentleman. He was scarcely nineteen when – on the
information of a lady – he was arrested as a spy. He was imprisoned in the Bastille where he wrote his first great comedy:
The Provok'd Wife. One cannot help wondering if the circum-
stance of his arrest influenced his choice of a title?

Certainly, he equalled Wycherley in sheer comedy (one's heart
goes out to the man who could write: 'Once a woman has given
you her heart, you can never get rid of the rest of her'); but he
lacked Wycherley's edge of criticism and vigorous attacks on
folly. But then Vanbrugh was an architect as well as a playwright; and there never was an architect yet possessed of much
power of criticism. A man needs to keep a straight face to build a
house; the possibility of folly must no more deflect his thoughts
than affect his foundations. There isn't much room for wit in
bricks and mortar – though occasionally they may be the cause
of it. When Voltaire visited Vanbrugh's massive palace of Blen-
heim, he remarked that if only the rooms had been as wide as
the walls were thick, the château would have been convenient
enough. Poor Vanbrugh! Even in death he was unable to escape
criticism of his massive style. His epitaph unkindly reads: 'Under
this stone, Reader survey, Dead Sir John Vanbrugh's house of
clay. Lie heavy on him, Earth! for he Laid many heavy loads on
thee!'

Beside William Wycherley hangs the gentleman to whom went
the lion's share of his artistic inheritance. William Congreve
smiles, not quite wholeheartedly, as he stands in a landscape
curiously inappropriate to one who 'nauseated country walking'
(see colour plate 5). If a single play could be picked out and held
up for admiration as the finest of the age – and, maybe the best
outside of Shakespeare – that play would surely be William
Congreve's *Way of the World*. The smile on his face – more the
shadow of a smile than the thing itself, suggests he is meditating
on his own words: 'It is the business of the comic poet to paint

the vices and follies of human kind.' His hand points across the landscape; his finger is crooked, almost as though he'd been unable to decide between beckoning and dismissal. Curious – that finger. The pose suggests a confusion in the painter's mind between the elegant gentleman before him and the traditional pose of John the Baptist. Had he perhaps sensed something prophetic about Congreve? All artists are prophets, and most of all the comic ones. More than a hundred years before Charles Darwin proposed *On the Origin of Species*, Congreve declared: 'I confess freely to you, I could never look long upon a monkey without very mortifying reflections.'

Very like his predecessor, Wycherley, he attacked the well-bred concealment of affection and the hypocrisy of the fashionable heart. In his masterpiece he makes Millament say to Mirabell, 'Let us be very strange and well-bred: let us be as strange as if we had been married a great while; and as well-bred as if we were not married at all.'

A last look at him, then, pointing out, with sovereign amusement and contempt – the Way of the World.

Not very far from William Congreve, but lower down on the wall, is an engraving of a man wearing an enormous, very curly wig; so large is this hairpiece in proportion to his head that one suspects he bought it second-hand from a giant. Such a wig might have fitted the huge head of a Bunyan. What lies under it? What, in short, is keeping it from extinguishing the wearer entirely? The fact that this is an engraving rather than a rich painting in oils suggests that the sitter did not have twenty guineas to spare for a Sir Godfrey Kneller; and there was no one prepared to pay it on his behalf. Yet, by reason of having been engraved, it would seem that this man's likeness was in popular demand. But he does not look popular. His expression is sour, his nose is long and keen; here is a man not given to frivolity, a man more inclined to see the world as an adversary rather than a friend (see plate 24).

'A middle-sized spare man about forty years old, of a brown complexion and dark brown coloured hair, but, wears a wig; a hooked nose, a sharp chin, grey eyes, and a large mole near his

24. Daniel Defoe

mouth.' This description of the man appeared in 1702 and even offered a reward for his apprehension. He was in demand in more ways than one. His particular crime had been the authorship of a pamphlet attacking the church for its way with Dissenters. He was caught, tried and sentenced to be exposed in the pillory and subsequently imprisoned. However, instead of the bricks and refuse ordinarily hurled at pilloried malefactors, this man was pelted with flowers. He was, in the truest sense of the word, a popular man.

So what was he? A London tradesman's son, a passionate Nonconformist who fought against King James II in the rebellion of 1685; a hosiery merchant who went bankrupt to the tune of £17,000 . . . and yet paid it all back; a vigorous, sturdy, latter-day Puritan, a political journalist, a government agent, a newspaper proprietor (who wrote himself every word he printed), and, at the age of forty, a gaol-bird. While in gaol, he, like the good journalist he was, wrote a description of the great storm in London of November, 1703. This is an extract from that description:

> Such a shock was given to a well-built house in the skirts of the city, by a stack of chimneys falling on the next houses, that the inhabitants imagined it was just coming down on their heads; but opening the door to attempt an escape into a garden, the danger was so apparent that they all thought fit to surrender to the disposal of Almighty Providence, and expect their graves in the ruin of their house, rather than meet most certain destruction in the open garden; for, unless they could have gone above 200 yards from any building, there had been no security; for the force of the wind blew the tiles point-blank, though their weight inclined them downward; and in several broad streets, the windows were broken by the flying of tile-sherds from the other side, and, where there was room for them to fly, tiles were blown above 30 or 40 yards, and stuck from 5 to 8 inches into the solid earth. Pieces of timber, iron, and sheets of lead, from higher buildings, were blown much farther.

This was written inside the prison, from where the writer could have seen absolutely nothing; yet such was the precision of his imagination, that it carries all the force of an eye-witness . . . and one equipped with instruments of measuring as well. At the age of sixty, when most men of his time would have been in the

grave or so deep in retirement that the distinction would have
been notional, this man exercised his extraordinary gift to an
unparalleled extent and wrote *The Life and Strange Surprising
Adventures of Robinson Crusoe*. His name was Daniel Defoe.
Following in that other Puritan gaol-bird's footsteps, John
Bunyan, Defoe created the second great prose work in English,
written to hearten and entertain the people. How strange it is
that these Puritans found optimism in their despair – while
others found only despair. Perhaps Defoe was right when he
said that 'A great man without religion is no more than a great
beast without a soul.'

In his most famous work, Defoe depicts man – ordinary,
commonplace man – as an individual with no one, no king,
prince or duke, between himself and his God; he shows him
surviving methodically, successfully and, ultimately happily in a
world that offers nothing unearned.

He wrote to be believed, and no one has ever succeeded better;
Robinson Crusoe is immeasurably more real than the shadowy
memoirs on which the author drew. Three years after *Robinson
Crusoe*, he wrote *Moll Flanders*, the marvellous *Journal of the
Plague Year* and *Colonel Jack*. He died – under slightly mysterious circumstances – at the age of seventy-two, having earned
the fair fortune he was possessed of by his pen alone. 'Writing,
you know,' he said, 'is become a very considerable branch of
the English Commerce.'

Charles Lamb said of Defoe's work that 'It is like reading
evidence in a Court of Justice.' Defoe would have liked that.
He always wrote – fact or fiction – as though on oath; and no one
has ever called him a perjurer.

So there they are – all these men, risen up out of the shadows of
earlier times, posturing, smiling, gesticulating and above all
rejoicing in their achievements and individual dignity. See how
they press upon the House of Hanover; some are only on the
steps, others already in the hallway. Which of their voices will
be heard to best effect? Congreve with his wit and elegance?
Defoe with his forthright realism? Will it be Locke and Newton,

turning all to system and method and confining the imagination to the strictly useful and commonsensical? Will the window that Defoe began to open on the street be pushed wider yet? Perhaps the genius of the age will turn to music and claim the inheritance of Henry Purcell; or will painting be the chief art of the new years and produce an English Rembrandt or Botticelli? Above all, will the common man continue to emerge from the shadows until he stands, 'warts and all', an equal among equals? This is the ideal. Politics can provide the stage; but without art – which provides the text – all that can ensue is dumb-show, riot and revolution.

In the very first year of the reign of the very first tenant of the House of Hanover, was passed the Riot Act. A significant piece of legislation. The passing of laws by governments reflects, all too clearly, the popular activities of the time. A careful study of the Ten Commandments will yield a shrewder picture of the ancient Israelites than all the work of diggers in the sand and gluers up of potsherds put together. Discover what those in office legislate against, and you will discover what most people are doing. They were rioting. The silk-weavers were rioting; the coal-heavers were rioting; the sailors were rioting, and so were the powdered footmen; the very gaol-birds of Newgate rioted – and gave the Sheriff of London gaol-fever of which he died. The tailors, being of a more peaceable or perhaps nervous disposition, humbly petitioned for better wages, and so did the stay-makers and the master hat-makers too. It was intolerable; everyone wanted more money for no better reason than that they needed it. Turbulence was in the air and ran along the black and filthy streets. Turned off soldiers from Marlborough's foreign wars applied their military skills to the home front by robbing coaches and sedan-chairs with a boldness and courage surpassing their energy in battle. A band of villains planned to enfilade George II's Queen in St Paul's churchyard; but, at the last moment, Divine Providence acting on behalf of the British Crown, sent a fat rich alderman rolling by – and they robbed him instead.

In short, it was the beginning of the modern world, with the

all-too-common man rising up with a wholly unacceptable
rapidity. The Riot Act was read more frequently than the Lord's
Prayer – and a good deal more devoutly too.

What a chance there was at such a time, with massive energies
on the boil and seething over, for something more illum-
inating than the Riot Act and its train of little paragraphs, to be
provided.

From the time of Queen Elizabeth – scarcely a hundred and
fifty years before – the culture of the land, which has always
been chiefly literary, had divided itself into two unequal streams.
The first, and immeasurably the larger, was Classical, deriving
itself from the ancient Greeks; the other was popular and sprang
from the English Bible, which was open to all. Although the
culture of ancient Greece had once been the property of a whole
people, the very antiquity of its language restricted it to scholars
and those who could afford to employ them. Even Greek sculp-
ture and architecture, that required no learning to admire,
became the spiritual furniture only of those with the time and
means to travel and behold them. So the stream along which an
artist sailed was determined by wealth and influence or the lack
of them; there was nothing innate about it; no man is ever born
refined. Inigo Jones – humble in origins – was given the opportunity to travel in Italy and brought back Classical architecture
to enrich his native land. A nobleman might well have come back
with a horse. Opportunity is all. Even now, should we not shudder
and weep to think of how many Shakespeares and Rembrandts
have lived and died in the prison of a vagrant's rags?

There was no want of artists in the Classical stream; the age
was stuffed with them. But with the best will in the world – and
many had it – they could provide no illumination for men who
were emerging from the dark; warlike and wondering. Down the
popular stream – which should have been the broader of the two
(if two there must be) – there had only sailed Shakespeare, held
in low repute with his 'small Latin and less Greek'; and John
Bunyan, whose *Pilgrim's Progress* had not yet emerged from 'the
cottage and the servants' hall'. Daniel Defoe, it's true, had made
some progress towards uniting the streams; it was no disgrace to

be found reading *Robinson Crusoe*; even though no gentleman was partial to its Dissenting tradesman author.

The gallery darkens – or, to be more exact, the light diminishes in quality. The very first room of the Hanoverian Succession has a twilit, dusty air, as of a respectable but none too frequented antique shop on the outskirts of a provincial town. The pictures have that indefinably second-hand look of things sold up by order of executors. To be honest, had they been on sale, one would not have been tempted to offer above twenty pounds . . .

> The general purpose of this paper is to expose the false arts of life, to pull off the disguises of cunning, vanity, and affectation, and to recommend a general simplicity in our dress, our discourse, and our behaviour.

Who said that? That gentleman over there – the fleshy one with the dark wig and leaning beside a frowzy-looking tree. Despite Knellerization, he looks irremediably plebeian.

> I shall be ambitious to have it said of me that I have brought philosophy out of closets and libraries, schools and colleges, to dwell in clubs and assemblies, at tea-tables and in coffee-houses.

Who said that? The gentleman hanging below the other; the rather elegant one, wearing a newly washed wig and the slightly shocked expression of one who has overheard a lady swearing.

This is Joseph Addison (see plate 25); above him lounges his partner in words, Sir Richard Steele (see plate 26). Between them, they virtually created the journal – the magazine. Theirs was the *Spectator*, that, from 1711, discoursed daily, in well-turned essays, on the follies and foibles of the age. Before them Daniel Defoe had produced his thrice-weekly newspaper, the *Review*, where, in addition to news and politics, there was a column known as 'The Scandal Club' in which manners and morality were criticized in terms Defoe had found to be popular. From this small portion of the labours of Daniel Defoe, Addison and Steele arose and, in the well-worn saying, 'delighted the town'.

Or at least, some ten thousand of the town (according to an estimate of the *Spectator*'s circulation); which, out of a popula-

25. Joseph Addison   26. Richard Steele

tion of close on a million, is as much as is generally meant by
'all the town'. (Much, much later, the phrase 'all London is
talking about it', certainly meant no more, and possibly, rather
less.) So perhaps Addison was wise in not following Socrates
entirely and bringing philosophy down from heaven to inhabit
among men; he contented himself with fetching it as far as the
fashionable tea-table. The *Spectator*'s very method of discourse
remained obstinately Classical; it followed Plato by inventing a
club whose members represented attitudes rather than human
beings: Sir Roger de Coverley, the country gentleman, Sir
Andrew Freeport, the City merchant, Will Honeycomb, the
man of style, etc., who debated on the superiority of Milton to
Homer and the propriety of giving cast-off clothing to a servant.
Truly the closet from which Joseph Addison fetched philosophy
was no great distance from the tea-table to which he brought it.
Daniel Defoe, had he judged it worth the labour of bringing,
would have fetched it into the tavern and the market place, to
take its chance with the ordinary talk of men.

Yet, here and there in the elegant bulk of the *Spectator*, occur
small items – generally the work of fleshy, plebeian-looking Dick

Steele – that suggest a broader view and a larger illumination might have been forthcoming, had there been encouragement. On Wednesday, 19 December, 1711, the following letter (by Steele) appeared:

> Dear Mr Spectator, I have a Sot of a Husband that lives a very scandalous Life, and wastes away his Body and Fortune in Debauches; and is immoveable to all the Arguments I can urge to him. I would gladly know whether in some Cases a Cudgel may not be allowed as a good Figure of Speech, and whether it may not be lawfully used by a female Orator.
>
> Your humble servant, Barbara Crabtree.

And on Friday, 28 December of the same year:

> Mr Spectator, Here's a Gentlewoman lodges in the same House with me, that I never did any Injury to in my whole Life; and she is always railing at me to those that she knows will tell me of it. Don't you think she is in Love with me? or would you have me break my Mind yet or not?
>
> Your servant, T.B.

Which is followed by,

> Mr Spectator,
>   I am a Footman in a great Family, and am in Love with the House-maid. We were all at Hot-cockles last Night in the Hall these Holi-days; when I lay down and was blinded, she pulled off her Shoe, and hit me with the Heel such a Rap, as almost broke my head to Pieces. Pray, Sir, was this Love or Spite?   T.

Is it not wonderful to think that our modern 'advice to the lovelorn' has such elderly and Classical roots?

So Addison and Steele, and many a lesser light, laboured for the gratification and applause of their ten thousand, who were 'all the town', which was, in effect, all the world. The rest were nobodies. In the *Covent Garden Journal*, NOBODY is satirically defined as 'all the people in Great Britain, except about 1,200'. And them, all in London, the middle of the civilized world. Nobodies: the countryman, the dull squires and their pudding wives; the trading classes and below them the labouring classes, the begging classes, the thieving and murdering classes, the hungry classes, the dying-in-the-streets and under-the-hedgerow classes. Nobodies . . . all the people in Great Britain except about 1,200 – or, to be generous, the *Spectator*'s 10,000. None the less, even this ten thousand was an immeasurably larger world than the one of so brief a time before when no man ever got out of the shadows without the help of a crown. If so much – and it *was* much! – had been accomplished in little more than a hundred and fifty years, what marvels must come next?

The chief purpose of art is to unite; whether in praise or criticism, in joy or anger, a union of minds and spirits is the underlying desire. Man is a pack animal; his deepest feelings are related to the instincts of the herd. Even those rare, eccentric artists who embark on solitary voyages of discovery of the soul, do so with the proud intention of returning and leading the adoring multitudes to 'fresh fields and pastures new'.

No one can deny that the arts of the age of Addison and Steele, Wren and Vanbrugh, Congreve and Sir Godfrey Kneller, united their world of ten thousand very satisfactorily. Admiration for and understanding of these arts became, as it were, a badge of breeding. Or would have done so had it not been more often the other way round. A badge of breeding tended to become a loud-voiced interest in the arts. For twenty guineas, one might obtain a Dedication and go down to posterity or, better, into one of the clubs, as a Patron and a Refined Man. So art and wealth became inseparable companions of the pocket; and artists being human (which has always been an expression denoting moral turpitude and generally the exhibition of those qualities that are not pleasant to think of as being human), rejoiced in the company they were keeping and felt no need to provide illumination beyond the windows of the mansions. It was, after all, infinitely more rewarding to design houses under the Palladian tutelage of the Earl of Burlington than to concern oneself with the workman's tenement and the labourer's cottage.

Look: there he lounges, the influential 3rd Earl (see plate 27) whose very name conjures up so tasteful and expensive a society

27. Third Earl of Burlington

that it is hard to believe that once Burlington House actually entertained real artists and even men of genius (see plate 28). Not, one hastens to say, in the person of the young earl himself whose talents lay rather in the direction of possessing sufficient

28. Burlington House, Piccadilly, London

taste to set himself up as a kind of wholesaler of talent, in the architectural, poetical and even the musical line.

Opposite the noble earl is fixed for ever (nothing seems closer to eternity than the arrangement of a picture gallery) one of his beneficiaries: a curious, not to say, inquisitive-looking fellow, who, like his patron, affects the loose night or day cap worn on the shaven head in place of the more formal wig. The face is lean and vaguely resentful . . . as if, without denying favours received, we would criticize the well-meaning nobleman for shutting him up in so comfortable a prison. And yet there is also, in that sharply intelligent face, an inward knowledge that some measure of blame is to be attached to the owner himself.

Dwarfish, brilliant, furiously ambitious, this is Alexander Pope – the very spirit of the age's poetry . . . which is no poetry at all but rhymed prose (see plate 29). Possessed of a facility in rhythm and words that amounted to genius, he was able to render down any man's thoughts, however unwieldy, into the neat dish of a couplet. Without Pope, dictionaries of quotations would go out of business (if it's neat, if it rhymes and if you've heard it before, it's Pope); he shaped genuine wisdom into little lozenges, most convenient for the mouths of after-dinner speakers, business men and fools.

How easy it is to declare that:

> Nature and Nature's laws lay hid in night:
> God said 'Let Newton be!' and all was light.

and not bother at all with the complicated achievement of the dour Sir Isaac himself.

The admirer and disciple of John Dryden, Pope excelled his master in daintiness of expression, but he lacked Dryden's passion and power. Dryden really cared about what he attacked; Pope was only concerned to have been seen in a hostile attitude. His frequent sharp remarks were more apt to redden the cheek than to draw blood. No gang of ruffians was ever hired to waylay Pope. His own ambition ever prevented him risking the serious displeasure of those his genius must have made him loathe and

5. William Congreve

6. Jonathan Swift

7. William Hogarth

8. Godfrey Kneller

9. Queen Caroline

29. Alexander Pope

despise. Deviousness was his besetting sin; if ever that discontent (which is the grain of sand that irritates the artist into producing a pearl), drove him to condemn a folly, an injustice,

an evil act, he did it so roundabout that only his closest friends
knew which way he'd been going at the time.

Yet Pope's face declares that he himself was no stranger to
his own failings and, at quiet times, helplessly raged against
them. 'This long disease, my life,' was said in no mood of pride
in achievement.

Once he committed the unpardonable folly of falling in love
with, and exposing his heart to that bitch of the first water (by
which I mean, bitch with a pedigree), Lady Mary Wortley
Montagu, who effortlessly ridiculed him for it. On closer
examination, Alexander Pope's countenance betrays the look of
a man who has had his aspirations flung in his face; of a man who,
in the unwelcome peace of his own company found himself
wondering if the game was worth the candle, when he himself
might have provided a brighter light for something more
enduring than a game.

30. Lady Montagu

By a shrewd stroke of irony, the bitch herself hangs some three yards off and no one marks her much. Lady Mary Wortley Montagu is represented in an eastern setting, drifting along beside a sexless child. Before her crouches a damsel playing an instrument that resembles a large soup spoon, while towards her, on the other side, an oriental person approaches, bearing a letter (see plate 30). Perhaps it is a letter from poor Pope?

When the gallery closes and the lights go out and the paintings come to life, does she take the letter eagerly and read it and look abashed? Does she smile pleadingly across the room and concede that time's verdict is juster than her own, that she was honoured by the friendship of men like Pope and not demeaned by it.

A very pretty, witty lady, a staunch upholder of women's – or, rather, ladies' rights, particularly the rights of ladies as pretty and witty as herself; the rights of others engrossed her rather less. She crumples up the letter, flings it to the ground and kicks it contemptuously aside with her foot, her face assumes a look of well-bred scorn as she declares that

> Imaginary humility has made me admit many familiar acquaintances of which I have heartily repented every one, and the greatest examples I have known of honour and integrity have been among those of the highest birth and fortunes.

She looks across the gallery and adds, without particular venom that

> By their birth and hereditary fortunes Dr Swift and Mr Pope deserved to be only a couple of footmen.

Born an Irishman, lived an Englishman, died a madman, Jonathan Swift sits in his study wrapped in his crumpled blue gown, with Aesop, Horace and Lucian for companions on the shelf behind him (see colour plate 6 and plate 31). He seems to have been interrupted in writing and looks not unkindly – as if a pleasant thought has just struck him. But there is something odd about the painting; and there was something odd about the man. The head seems more to be perching on the shoulders than to be growing from them. The cleric's Geneva bands

31. Jonathan Swift

hang down from below the full chin like a pair of folded wings
– for all the world as if about to spread themselves and carry
the intent face elsewhere. There is a contradiction . . .

As it is in the portrait, so it was with the sitter: never were
head and heart set at such odds with each other as in the person
of Dean Swift. One of the sharpest minds the world has ever

known found itself in harness with one of the most twisted, tormented hearts that seemed unable to express love save through the most appalling fury and hate. A lesser mind would have produced a monster; a wiser heart would have given us a genius saint.

'I have ever hated all nations, professions and communities, and all my love is towards individuals,' he wrote. 'But principally I hate and detest that animal called man, although I heartily love John, Peter, Thomas, and so forth. This is the system upon which I have governed myself many years . . . Upon this great foundation of misanthropy . . . the whole building of my Travels is erected; and I will never have peace of mind till all honest men are of my opinion.'

The Travels referred to are those of Lemuel Gulliver, a giant figure more than worthy to tread in the footsteps of Bunyan's Christian and Defoe's Crusoe. Like his great predecessors, Gulliver is Everyman, voyaging out among wonders. Although the conception of marvellous travels may have come from the Greek satirist, Lucian, and the precision with which they are described from Daniel Defoe, the mockery and rage with which they are informed is Swift's, and Swift's alone.

The first voyage to Lilliput – the kingdom of six-inch midgets – explores with blazing comedy the absurd self-importance and customs of human beings when viewed by the giant Gulliver. The second voyage, to Brobdingnag, the land of giants, reverses the satire and shows us man-sized Gulliver, indignantly defending his homeland and its statecraft against the bewilderment and withering scorn of the king of the giants, until that huge worthy:

> could not forbear taking me up in his right hand, and stroking me gently with the other, after an hearty fit of laughing, asked me, whether I were a Whig or a Tory.

But when Gulliver has gone more deeply into the history and laws of his homeland, the smile leaves the giant king's face and he is driven to declare that:

> I cannot but conclude the bulk of your natives to be the most pernicious race of little odious vermin that nature ever suffered to crawl upon the face of the earth.

Next, Gulliver voyages to Laputa and related lands where the excesses of scholarship and pedantry are mercilessly derided; but it is in the last voyage of all, to the land of horses, that Swift's fury bursts its bands so that some declared he was already mad when he wrote it. Here, in this country of gentle horses, called Houyhnhnms, he finds the Yahoos, who serve, in the most menial capacity, their masters, the wise horses. Upon the person of the Yahoos, Swift has lavished every vice and bestiality of which the human race is capable. It is a veritable paeon of loathing for his own kind.

Yet to leave Dean Swift with the taste only of his hatreds, is to be monstrously unjust. Consider, instead, the woman he loved more deeply than any soul alive; consider his 'Stella'. Could not the portrait represent the Sunday evening when he received the news of Stella's death and he resolved to sit down and write about her, in exact terms, setting down all her qualities with agonizing dispassion, as if, by so doing, he could alleviate the intolerable pain her death occasioned:

> This day, being Sunday, January 28, 1727–8, about eight o'clock at night, a servant brought me a note, with an account of the death of the truest, most virtuous, and valuable friend that I, or perhaps any other person, was ever blessed with. She expired about six in the evening of this day; and as soon as I am left alone, which is about eleven at night, I resolve, for my own satisfaction, to say something of her life and character.
>
> She was born in Richmond, in Surrey, on the thirteenth day of March, in the year 1681. Her father was a younger brother of a good family in Nottinghamshire, her mother of a lower degree; and indeed she had little to boast of her birth. I knew her from six years old, and had some share in her education, by directing what books she should read, and perpetually instructing her in the principles of honour and virtue; from which she never swerved in any one action or moment of her life. She was sickly from her childhood until about the age of fifteen; but then grew into perfect health, and was looked upon as one of the most beautiful, graceful, and agreeable young women in London, only a little too fat.

Mark that expression: 'only a little too fat'. Conceive the despairing smile with which it must have been set down. Surely it must take its place beside King Lear's: 'Pray you undo this button', uttered in the extremity of his stupendous grief. It is by such uncanny flashes of simplicity, unerringly placed, that the greatest artists can, as if by witchcraft, poke their fingers through flesh and bone and touch, actually *touch*, the undefended heart.

> Her hair was blacker than a raven, and every feature of her face in perfection . . .
>
> January 29. My head aches, and I can write no more.
>
> January 30. Tuesday. This is the night of the funeral, which my sickness will not suffer me to attend. It is now nine at night, and I am removed into another apartment, that I may not see the light in the church, which is just over against the window of my bed-chamber.

He continues, quietly, methodically, setting down every quality of Stella, as if to bring her into the chamber where he sits:

> But she had another quality that much delighted her, although it may be thought a kind of check upon her bounty; however it was a pleasure she could not resist: I mean that of making agreeable presents; wherein I never knew her equal, although it be an affair of as delicate a nature as most in the course of life. She used to define a present: That it was a gift to a friend of something he wanted, or was fond of, and which could not be easily gotten for money.

In 1738, his sickness became more apparent, in violent headaches and attacks of giddiness. Grimly, whenever he took leave of friends, he said: 'Goodnight, I hope I shall never see you again.' In 1742 guardians were appointed to look after him; in 1745 he died, having been in a state of enfeebled madness for three years. Among his deathbed possessions was a lock of Stella's hair, inscribed: 'Only a woman's hair'.

Thackeray says of him: 'An immense genius: an awful downfall and ruin. So great a man he seems, that thinking of him is like an empire falling.'

* * *

In a letter to his good friend Pope, Swift once asked: 'What think you of a Newgate Pastoral?' Presumably Pope didn't think too much of it; but mercifully, another friend of Swift's – one John Gay – thought otherwise. The Newgate Pastoral emerged, in 1728, as *The Beggar's Opera*.

During the writing of this remarkable piece, Gay read his work in progress to Swift and Pope (awesome thought!) and doubtless received many hints, it being contrary to the nature of authors to refrain from giving advice to colleagues. Perhaps it was Swift who proposed the violently satirical nature of the work – representing Sir Robert Walpole as Peachum, etc. – but the immense vigour and essentially popular nature of *The Beggar's Opera* is something removed a little from the Classicism of Pope and Swift. To all intents a new form of popular art had been created, and from the most refractory materials. The wit and satire of Gay's two great friends are united with the 'low-life' representations of Defoe's Moll Flanders and together they find a glorious richness and vitality in the company of the music of the cottage and tavern. (For his tunes, Gay looked no further than a compilation of popular airs published some years before under the title of *Wit and Mirth*.) So deep in every heart was the music of *The Beggar's Opera* that it was said of it that it was the only entertainment where everyone went *into* the theatre humming the airs. (Everyone . . . who was everyone? Still the same 10,000? Most likely. It would seem that when God made the world He'd divided it between Everyman and Neveryman. Neveryman, I will *not* go with thee, and be thy guide. You must just tag along behind and catch what you can as the world of art and culture goes rolling on ahead.)

The musical fashion of the time had been for Italian opera, which fashion Joseph Addison had attacked most wittily in the *Spectator*, for its incomprehensibility to the general run of audiences who knew no Italian. Addison's indignation over the failure of music to reach the common Englishman had not been unconnected with the failure of his own opera, *Rosomond*, to do that very thing; nevertheless, his point had been just. But the most powerful weapon against a fashion is not merely to laugh

at it, but to provide a better. This Gay did, and before the blast
of this tale of highwaymen, pimps, gaolers and prostitutes, Italian
opera withered away. More than anything, it was the infusion of
popular culture that made *The Beggar's Opera* the masterpiece
it is. Gay's original idea had been to have no accompaniments to
the tunes but to allow them to rise naturally and unsupported
from the speech in the way a man might hum to himself or a
child might burst into song. But he was talked out of this stroke
of genius and persuaded to enlist the aid of Dr Pepusch, a
German musician who, in the words of Dr Burney, the musical
historian

> composed an original overture upon the subject of one of the tunes
> and furnished the wild, rude, and often vulgar melodies, with bases
> so excellent, that no sound contrapuntist will ever attempt to alter
> them.

It is the common habit of human beings, when they have come
out of a dark place and have got over blinking at the light, to set
about criticizing what they see. Thus, on a domestic level, when
a couple have been out to dinner in the house of a rich acquaintance, the chief of their homeward talk is generally devoted to
abusing their host's taste by discussing how much better his
wealth might have been laid out in more judicious hands – such
as their own. So it was on the grander level: poets, playwrights
and satirists, enjoying their freedom, attacked the falsity and
rank corruption they saw directly above them. There was a
marvellous sharpness of eye in detecting pox in the duchess,
lechery in the minister and skeletons in the most respected
closets; but there was not – save for fleeting instances – an equal
sharpness in spying out the skeletons in the tenements and the
running sores in the streets. Although *The Beggar's Opera* displayed the vice in the streets and in the gaols, it contained not
one ounce of pity.

Sometimes it seems that the whole huge business of art,
weaving its endless, serpentine way through time, is like a children's game in which a whisper is passed from lip to ear down a

birthday party, until it comes out, wonderfully changed by reason of things half heard and deficiencies made up out of the imagination of each listener. 'Corruption in high places', whispers John Gay, who got it, in part, from Pope and Swift; 'the only honest trade is to be a thief', he adds, partly of his own and partly a garbled echo of Daniel Defoe.

'Corruption', hears William Hogarth, the greatest of all English artists; but, by reason of turning to look about him, finishes the sentence otherwise as he sees corruption in low places, also.

He perches on a shelf in a gallery that adjoins the twilit domain of Swift, Pope, Addison and Steele. He is done in terracotta, by the French sculptor, Roubiliac (see colour plate 7). The face is as real as yours or mine . . . and ten times sharper in its sudden turn to note down some passing curiosity. Perhaps it was no more than an interest in the sculptor's technique; or, more likely, it was to make a mental note – in the mysterious internal shorthand of which he alone was master – of the curved lines that went to make up some tabby cat intent on crime, such as he delighted to include in his great family portraits and conversation pieces.

Having been born and spent a humble childhood close by Newgate Gaol, the world of *The Beggar's Opera* takes on a reality somewhat less comic than John Gay's. Scenes of terror and degradation must have been deep in his memory. He hears Gay mention 'thief', and once more cannot help looking about him to see that thieves are not only Ministers of the Crown, but men and women, too, who had grown out of fearfully nurtured children that littered the streets like sharp, malicious rats. Pity consumes him, and what he passes on (in this whispering game of art), is something changed from what he's taken in.

One of Hogarth's first paintings in oils was of a scene from *The Beggar's Opera*. The stage always attracted Hogarth powerfully, and in Gay's great work – which demanded a style of acting more naturalistic than the formal comedies of Wycherley and Congreve – he found that close relation to life that enriched his imagination. This painting was executed in 1728; thereafter he divided his talents between fashionable groups for the rising middle class, and the engravings which he produced in large numbers, to be sold for some three shillings a time to the huge public of the poor that never before had been thought of as a worthy audience for art. It is on these engravings, and the intention behind them, that Hogarth's claim to greatness rests; and most of all on the astonishing series of pictures on single subjects that were, in effect, deeply moving stories, related half like plays and half like novels, but enlivened in every corner by the painter's eye. The first of these was 'The Harlot's Progress', published in 1732. George Vertue, the engraver and collector, describes how it came about:

> The most remarkable subject of painting that captivated the minds of most people, persons of all ranks and conditions from the greatest quality to the meanest, was the story painted and designed by Mr Hogarth of 'The Harlot's Progress' and the prints engraved by him and published.
>
> Amongst other designs of his in painting he began a small picture of a common harlot, supposed to dwell in Drury Lane, just rising about noon out of bed and at breakfast . . . This whore's deshabille, careless and a pretty countenance and air – this thought pleased many. Some advised him to make another to it as a pair, which he did. Then other thoughts increased and multiplied by his fruitful invention, till he made six different subjects which he painted so naturally, the thoughts, and so striking the expressions that it drew everybody to see them – which he proposing to engrave in six plates to print, at one guinea each set, he had daily subscriptions came in, in fifty or a hundred pounds a week.

Of all Hogarth's series of engravings, the most powerful is 'The Four Stages of Cruelty'. In the four tableaux that constitute the series, he depicts, with merciless clarity, the progress of a child – one Tom Nero of the Parish of St Giles – from street urchin to the hanged felon in the dissecting theatre of the Barber-Surgeons Company in Monkwell Street (see plates 32a, b, c and d).

In the first engraving, Tom Nero, as a child, is seen mercilessly torturing a dog, while round about him children are to be seen

While various Scenes of sportive Woe
The Infant Race employ,
And tortur'd Victims bleeding shew
The Tyrant in the Boy.
Design'd by W. Hogarth

Behold a Youth of gentler Heart,
To spare the Creature's pain
O take, he cries—take all my Tart,
But Tears and Tart are vain.
Published according to Act of Parliament Nov. 1. 1751.

Learn from this fair Example—You
Whom savage Sports delight,
How Cruelty disgusts the view
While Pity charms the sight.
Price 1.ˢ

32a. 32b. 32c. 32d. The Four Stages of Cruelty by William Hogarth

indulging in every species of cruelty imaginable towards helpless animals in the street.

In the second engraving, Tom Nero, now grown to manhood, is a coachman thrashing a fallen horse. Once again, the streets

The generous Steed in hoary Age
Subdu'd by Labour lies;
And mourns a cruel Master's rage,
While Nature Strength denies.

The tender Lamb o'er drove and faint,
Amidst expiring Throws;
Bleats forth its innocent complaint
And dies beneath the Blows.

Inhuman Wretch! say whence proceeds
This coward Cruelty?
What Intrest springs from barbrous deeds?
What Joy from Misery?

Designed by W. Hogarth.   Published according to Act of Parliament Feb 1 1751.

abound with cruelty, committed no longer by children, but by the men into which they have grown. Notices on the walls advertise prize-fighting and cock-fighting, and a dozing drayman lets his laden cart run across the body of a screaming child who has been playing with a hoop.

The third engraving shows Tom Nero arrested for the murder

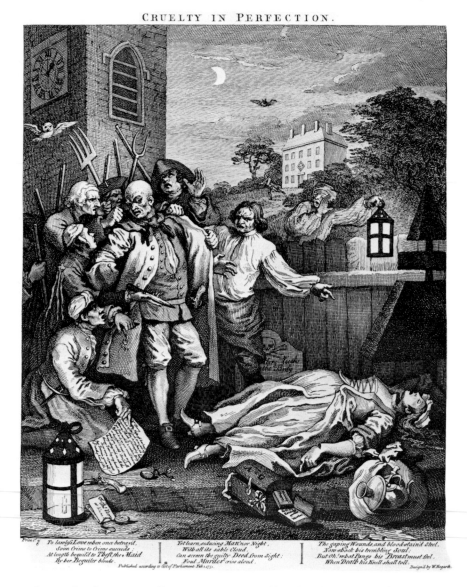

Price 6d.

To lawless Love when once betray'd,
Soon Crime to Crime succeeds:
At length beguil'd to Theft, the Maid
By her Beguiler bleeds.

Yet learn, seducing Man! nor Night,
With all its sable Cloud,
Can screen the guilty Deed from Sight:
Foul Murder cries aloud.

The gaping Wounds, and blood-stain'd Steel,
Now shock his trembling Soul:
But Oh! what Pangs his Breast must feel,
When Death his Knell shall toll.

Published according to Act of Parliament Feb.1.1751.

Design'd by W.Hogarth.

of a pathetic accomplice, one Ann Gull, who lies at his feet with her throat cut and her hand almost hacked off, indicating the violence of the struggle that ended in her death. There is no want of cruelty in the faces of those who have seized the murderer; the victim alone wears the face of innocence.

The last of the series is the most horrifying of all, as Tom

THE REWARD OF CRUELTY.

Price 1s. Behold the Villain's dire disgrace!   Torn from the Root, that wicked Tongue,   His Heart, expos'd to prying Eyes, Design'd by W.Hogarth
        Not Death itself can end.   Which daily smore and curst!   To Pity has no Claim:
        He finds no peaceful Burial-Place;   Those Eyeballs from their Sockets wrung, But, dreadful from his Bones shall rise,
         His breathless Corse, no friend.   That glow'd with lawless Lust;   His Monument of Shame.
                                   Published according to Act of Parliament Feb.1 1751.

Nero, looking dreadfully alive, is being torn to scientific pieces
by surgeons who look no less bestial than the hanged man himself.
Two skeletons seem to look on from alcoves beside the windows.
One of them is the remains of John Field, a prize-fighter whose
contest had been advertised on the wall in the second engraving.
He, like Tom Nero, had been hanged. Hogarth knew full well

the violence that is embedded in sport. On the floor, beside the dissecting table, a dog eats Tom Nero's heart.

Hogarth's anger matches Swift's; not even in the last voyage of Gulliver is there more savagery displayed; but there is more than anger here. There is a deep concern for the plight of men, reared in a sort of hell. And, above all, there is a passionate concern for children. Although Hogarth frequently depicts the young as cruel and vicious, he never fails to depict them as the victims of example and the lack of guidance. Of this series, Hogarth himself said:

> The prints were engraved with the hope of in some degree correcting the barbarous treatment of animals the very sight of which renders the streets of our Metropolis so distressing to every feeling mind. If they have had that effect and checked the progress of cruelty, I am more proud of having been the author, than I should be of having painted Raffaelle's Cartoons.

The window that Daniel Defoe had begun to open on the street that lay beyond the palace and the mansion's parlour, had been flung wide by William Hogarth. It is a measure of his power that his very name has been taken to sum up the age. This honour, of giving his name to an age, he shares with kings. Thus, while the architecture and silver of the time are called 'Georgian', after the dim procession of Georges who occupied the throne, the people are called 'Hogarthian', after the artist who never wavered in his concern for them. When Captain Coram, that kindly sea-captain, struggled to establish his Hospital for Foundlings, it was to William Hogarth (among others), that he applied for approval and help.

This Captain Coram was one of those rare men in whom the critical spirit of the times had matured enough to lose its sourness. Deeply moved by the daily sight of infants abandoned in the streets by their husbandless mothers, he resolved, on his retirement from the sea, to devote his life to providing a home for them. At first, the captain was sternly opposed by those who declared that assistance to illegitimate children amounted to encouragement to the immorality that had brought them into being. But, little by little, over many years, he gained sufficient support and, in 1747, the Foundling Hospital opened its doors for business. The first two foundlings were named Thomas and Eunice Coram, after the captain and his wife; who, doubtless, regarded it as an honour received rather than one bestowed. To begin with, the Hospital no less than the Foundlings, had teething problems: unmarried mothers crowded the gates, pushing their infants through the bars in their anxiety not to be too late. Clearly something had to be done, so the women were admitted to a waiting room where lots were drawn to determine which infants should be saved. In time, however, this judgement of Solomon was mitigated into a sensible investigation of each applicant's need.

Among the first governors of the Foundling Hospital, needless to say, was William Hogarth. He gave his great painting, 'The March to Finchley', to the Hospital to be auctioned, and, in addition, gave them the unsold tickets. The Hospital won the painting and, to the artist's pleasure, kept it in a place of honour. He took his duties seriously; he and his wife being childless, they took some of the children into their own home to give them the most hopeful start in life. So perhaps it is only fitting that, while the Georges were immortalized in tea-pots and commodes, this, their humble subject, should be immortalized in human beings.

Although by the time that Hogarth's finest works were being done, the first King George had long since died and given way, unnoticeably, to the second, one supposes he had such an artist in mind, together with such authors as Swift and Gay, when he made what was one of his few remarks in English, and certainly one of the last public utterances on the arts made by a reigning British monarch. 'I hate all Boets and Bainters,' he said; and doubtless clutched at his fat German mistresses as if in defence. So – 'Boets and Bainters' were out; that left, by default, musicians. The portly monarch was reputed to be fond of music. Well, well, one supposes he had to be fond of something. Most of the prince-lings who ruled over the cheek by jowl German and Austrian courts supported music, which was an art that required neither the intellectual effort of reading, nor was able to make irreverent fun of Personages – and supplied an agreeable noise to take the place of conversation. It was, in every respect, a Royal art. It became quite the thing to have a better band and more talented concertmaster than one's neighbouring crowned head. In this way a species of Royal taste came into being, and George I – one-time Elector of Hanover – came to England in 1714 with half a dozen mistresses and a reputation for being musical (see plate 33).

Unfortunately England did not have the same rivalry between next-door courts, so 'Bainters' and more particularly 'Boets', whose work was addressed to a wide audience had flourished rather more than had musicians. 'Bainters' had never done quite so well, lacking, as they did in a Protestant land, the patronage and inspiration of the Catholic church. It was difficult for an artist to bring the same degree of enthusiasm to the enrichment of a man's house as he might to God's.

George I did not like England. There were too many people, and they all spoke the wrong language. He took every opportunity of waddling, at high speed, back to Hanover, leaving England in the public-spirited (and pocketed) hands of Sir Robert Walpole, the first Prime Minister. It was totally beyond royal comprehension that anyone who could go to Hanover should stay in England. The fact that an employee of his, to whom he had generously granted a few months' leave from Hanover some three years previously, had gone to London and was still there, as if he had a right to be, must have both baffled and irritated him.

The employee himself must have been no less disturbed to find the monarch he had absconded from was, all of a sudden, on the throne of the land he had absconded to. There is a tale told of how George Frideric Handel made his apologies for his oversight in not returning to Hanover. Charles Burney records it:

> Handel, conscious of his deficiency in respect and gratitude . . . durst not approach the Court . . . the King, soon after his arrival in these kingdoms, having been prevailed on to form a party on the

33. George I

water, the design was communicated to Handel who was advised to compose some pieces expressly for the occasion; the performance of which he secretly conducted in a boat that accompanied the royal barge. Upon hearing these compositions, which have been since so well known and so justly celebrated under the title of the 'Water Music', His Majesty, equally surprised and pleased by their excellence, eagerly enquired who was the author of them; when the Baron acquainted the King that they were the production of a faithful servant of His Majesty, who, conscious of the cause of displeasure which he had given to so gracious a protector, durst not presume to approach his royal presence till he had assurances that by every possible demonstration of duty and gratitude in future, he might hope to obtain a pardon. This intercession having been graciously accepted, Handel was restored to favour . . .

This grand party – and grand it must have been if the magnificence of the music is a guide – took place on 17 July, 1717. Handel, at that time, was a much-travelled thirty-two. He had been born in Halle (in the same year as Bach), of markedly unmusical parents, travelled to Berlin and Hamburg and then to Italy, where he took what suited him from Italian music before returning to Germany and taking employment with the court of Hanover.

A great mystery has always been made as to why Handel came to London. Most likely he heard that the Italian opera was making a fortune there; men have travelled to stranger places for lesser reasons than commercial success. What matters is that Handel came to England, and, to the everlasting credit of England, he became an Englishman. To argue that he was a German, merely because he'd been born in Halle, is as sensible as arguing (as the saying goes), that a cat born in a stable is necessarily a horse.

Nowadays, scholars have upset the tale of the 'Water Music'. 'Internal evidence' has discredited the word of both Mainwaring and Dr Charles Burney, both of whom knew the composer and, presumably, got it from him. Oh, well, internal evidence has done for Handel, too. This 'internal evidence' consists chiefly of the realization that the 'Water Music' comprises three distinct suites, composed at different times. To my mind it is like performing a post-mortem on a martyred saint, finding his liver diseased, and then declaring that 'internal evidence' proves that here was no good man. Such painstaking investigation may be the bread and butter of scholars; the trouble is, it steals everyone else's vehicle for jam.

There are always good stories about great men; they express something deeper and truer than facts. Somehow they enshrine those intangible feelings we all have about human beings blessed with powers bordering on the divine.

The child Handel, surprised in his stern father's attic, playing on his secret clavichord with miraculous skill, has something Biblical about it. The story of the seven-year-old boy running for miles after his father's coach and weeping to be taken to Halle (whence his father, a surgeon, was bound), and there playing on the Court chapel organ to the wonderment of all, has the quality of all great stories embedded in it.

In London, it's said, he was deeply in love twice; but on each occasion, the ladies – or their mothers – demanded he choose between music and marriage. How curious that they should seek to dispense with what had first drawn them. Confronted with this choice of Achilles, Handel chose music; there are no stories to suggest that he regretted it.

His great personal strength has been immortalized in the tale of his holding an errant soprano out of his window in Brook Street and threatening to drop her unless she sang in accordance with his music and not for her own vanity. If sopranos then were as sopranos now, Handel's feat places him in the company of Hercules. His profound understanding of the nature of singers is further remembered in the tale of the exasperated performer who, during a rehearsal, threatened to jump on the harpsichord unless Mr Handel refrained from criticizing him. To this, Handel replied that, if he could have advance notice of the event, he would gladly advertise it as the public would sooner pay to see him jump than hear him sing.

Such then, and many more, are the legends that have come to

surround this great man. They have their roots in affection and awe. To dismiss them all is to injure us, not him.

But for Handel's music, we need no legends. Its mixture of strength and tenderness, of nobility and ripe good humour places it, as Dr Burney says: 'out of the reach of time and fashion'.

So Handel came to London to write Italian operas and make his fortune. At first he prospered – and so did music, to the tunes of some forty operas, interspersed with sonatas, anthems, and one matchlessly beautiful masque, called *Acis and Galatea*, for which John Gay wrote the words.

But the Italian opera was opposed by a faction that sought to revive the style of the musical plays of Henry Purcell, as being more suited to the genius of the English people. Joseph Addison, in the *Spectator*, said a great many rude things about the Italian opera . . . and quite a few sensible ones as well. He went to the Haymarket Theatre to see *Armida*, by Handel, and discovered that:

> The King of Jerusalem is obliged to come from the City on foot, instead of being drawn in a triumphal Chariot by white Horses, as my Opera-book had promised me; and thus while I expected Armida's Dragons should rush forward towards Argantes, I found the Hero was obliged to go to Armida, and hand her out of her Coach. We had also but a very short Allowance of Thunder and Lightning; tho' I cannot in this place avoid doing Justice to the Boy who had the Direction of the two painted Dragons, and made them spit Fire and Smoke: He flashed out his Rosin in such just Proportions and in such due Time, that I could not forbear conceiving Hopes of his being one Day a most excellent Player. I saw indeed but Two things wanting to render his whole Action compleat, I mean the keeping his Head a little lower, and hiding his Candle . . . The Sparrows and Chaffinches at the Haymarket fly as yet very irregularly over the Stage; and instead of perching on the Trees and performing their Parts, these young Actors either get into the Galleries or put out the Candles . . .

But the chief of his abuse was levelled against the custom of putting a whole entertainment on the stage in a language the audience could not understand. I would like to be able to tell Joseph Addison that that particular folly has gone from us entirely; but the other day I went to a performance of *The Magic Flute*, given in its native German with all the dialogue, down to the last full stop. During this dialogue, which was badly acted as is the custom among opera singers, little gusts of laughter like puffs of smoke kept coming up from the audience (of whom maybe a hundredth part understood German), at jokes which, had they been in English, would have been scorned by a seaside comic.

In the late 1720s, when Italian opera was being laid in its grave and *The Beggar's Opera* was shovelling in the earth, Handel turned to the language of his adopted land and began to write the great oratorios – which are really English operas, removed from the incompetence of actors and the megalomania of producers. I've heard it said – by real scholars – that such dramatic master-pieces as *Saul*, *Samson* and *Susanna* cry out to be staged. Well, I once saw *Samson* presented so; and the spectacle of the majestic double chorus of Israelites and Philistines shaking their fists at one another in time to the music would have sent Addison flying for his pen.

Suddenly I paused in my gallery-wandering. I wanted to see this man – the first world-artist since Shakespeare to make his home in England. (Only Charles Dickens after him has aspired to the same eminence.) I was still by the bust of Hogarth. Surely Handel must be near? They'd been acquainted . . . I searched. No Handel. Perhaps I'd missed him? I went back to Swift and Pope and Lady Mary Wortley Montagu (who looked smaller than ever). No Handel. I walked through the Kit-Kat Club, which previously I'd avoided. Saw Sir Godfrey Kneller, looking like a genteel angel and delusively young. He had succeeded in Knellerizing himself (see colour plate 8). Round about him, the Club smiled convivially. What did its well-off members do? Drank, talked art and philosophy and played faro and whist (see plate 34). It was an age of Clubs. Man, from being a herd or pack animal, had developed into a pack-of-cards animal. I went

34. Two noble members of the Kit-Kat Club

on, through another archway. A fat man in brocade and holding a document, simpered at me as if he'd just cheated me out of a fortune and was defying me to discover how it had been done. Sir Robert Walpole, the first Prime Minister; every inch the politician – or should one say, statesman? What's the difference! A statesman is only a politician in hardback (see plate 35).

Next to him, King George II and Caroline, his admirable Queen (see colour plate 9). On the other side of the royal pair, in a matching frame, hangs – Good God! That can't be George Frideric Handel! Not that portly, dyspeptic-looking gent in tight blue velvet, with a sword at his side and his hat tucked underneath his arm. For all the world, he looks to be an uncomfortable caller on a Sunday afternoon who has been awkwardly deposited on the only empty seat, which happened

35. Sir Robert Walpole

to be at a side-table on which a copy of 'Messiah' had been inadvertently left (see plate 36 and colour plate 10).

'Have pity on him, sir. He was an old man, then. He was seventy-one, and nearly blind.'

My informant was my old friend, the attendant from

36. George Frideric Handel

downstairs, who'd emerged from a small annexe where he seemed to have been awaiting my arrival before the portrait of Handel.

'I see you took my tip, sir, and began at the beginning.'

I nodded and admitted grudgingly that the advice had been more fruitful than I'd supposed. He looked so pleased at this that I couldn't refrain from taking him into my confidence and imparting everything that had come into my head since that ancient time when I'd travelled by lift to Richard II.

'I like it, sir,' he said generously. 'I'd never have thought you could have made so much out of that little engraving of Daniel Defoe. It just shows, sir, what one can do when one puts one's mind to it. But I find it surprising you never breathed a word about Oliver Cromwell. Mr Defoe would have been disappointed in that.'

'I mentioned John Bunyan,' I said defensively. 'He was a representative Puritan, surely?'

'Ah yes. You did indeed. And very handsomely, sir. But, on the other hand, if you'll forgive another little tip . . . you skimped John Locke rather. I don't think you mentioned how much Daniel Defoe owed to him. After all, John Locke was a great one for clear style and using words properly and in accordance with what you know.'

I was about to ask if this information was a consequence of his attending evening classes in philosophy, but I felt it would be improper to mock his aspirations to learning, which were really very creditable.

However, he was more perceptive than I. Seeing my hesitation and divining its cause, he looked politely down at his black, shiny boots and remarked, half reproachfully and half apologetically, 'But we can't have everything, sir; and really I want to say how much I admire your notion of culture being divided between the Classical and the popular. Very interesting, that.'

'Yes, yes!' I put in quickly; and went on to develop the idea of how art, which was meant to unite, had become more and more estranged from the common people –

'With the exception, sir, as you so rightly pointed out, of the popular as represented by the Bible, Shakespeare, John Bunyan, Daniel Defoe and –'

'And Hogarth, of course!'

'I was going to say Hogarth, and *The Beggar's Opera*. All the same, I couldn't help noticing you had a good word to say for Dr Swift. Very Classical, the Dean, sir.'

'But with a strong influence of Daniel Defoe.'

'And John Locke, sir . . . if I might be so bold. All the same, I'm glad you haven't set your mind against the Classical altogether . . . even though it seems to leave people like me out in the dark – to use your own very apt image, sir.'

He smiled, without a trace of irony, and went on: 'Because I myself, sir, am very partial to a bit of John Milton, now and then: a Classical poet if ever there was one. Perhaps that's why you never mentioned Milton? Or did you miss him in walking through? He *is* rather tucked away; but we've a nice painting of him as a young man . . . the Lady of Christ's, they used to call him, on account of his delicate features (see plate 37). I should think the likeness was taken about the time he wrote:

> Quips and cranks and wanton wiles
> Nods and becks and wreathed smiles,
> Such as hang on Hebe's cheek
> And love to live in dimple sleek . . .

I'm sure I don't know who Hebe was, but it's a lovely piece, and I wouldn't want to be without it, even though it's not in the popular vein. D'you see, sir, there's a danger in fine humanitarianism, such as yours, that by the time you've brought us all into the light, you'll have cleared away all the things we were looking forward to seeing. Isn't it a pity, sir, that it had to be *The Beggar's Opera* instead of the Italian opera? Why couldn't it have been both? I don't think rivalry is ever a very healthy thing in the long run. One side always goes to the wall and so we've lost a half of our capital. Or, to put it another way, must we always throw out the baby with the bath water?'

'Casualties in the march of history,' I said, feeling rather pleased with the expression.

37. John Milton

'Ah! I see you are a follower of Tolstoy, sir. The forces that move nations, and all that.'

Confound these Adult Education classes! I thought; but refrained from saying so.

'But to follow your very apt image, sir,' went on the attendant, '(You *must* be literary, sir, if you'll forgive the observation!), isn't it the business of humanitarians and well-informed persons generally to succour the wounded and bring the casualties to safety?'

'Not when they're dead.'

'Elderly, sir. Aged, not dead. Art can't die; it can only be forgotten. Now according to a gentleman who came to talk to us the other night, our society is based on nurturing the young and caring for the old. To neglect either, he said, was to betray ourselves and reduce our own lives to a short and murderous prime. Do you know, sir, sometimes, before the visitors come in, and after they've gone, I stroll through the galleries and look at all our wise ladies and gentlemen who, in their time, considered this very world in which you and I live – and I feel very comforted by the company. Perhaps, sir, you would call it sitting by the roadside while history marches on? But I march too. I go to evening classes, watch television and talk with visitors such as yourself. No, sir; I don't see history as a march or a force. I think of it more as both a childhood and an old age, to be nurtured by some of us and cared for by others so that all of us may enjoy a longer, richer prime. After all, sir, the man without a memory is mad; and that's a fact. A people without a past, sir, are in much the same state.'

'Who does the nurturing and who does the caring?' I asked, a little confused.

'Why, sir, the historians do the caring, and the artists do the bringing up, in the way of good parents.'

'Each in his own image?'

The attendant who, all this while had been studying his boots, looked up and smiled. He glanced at the painting of Handel then, quite suddenly, excused himself; he was due elsewhere. However, he promised he'd be back as he was interested in my progress through space and time. With a last respectful look at the portrait, he left me, full of doubts which I tried to resolve by contemplating the worried, uncomfortable-looking composer of the 'Messiah'.

Who killed the Italian opera? I, said Joseph Addison; with my little pen. I, said John Gay; with my breath of a people's art. We, said the actors; with our brand-new, naturalistic acting.

I looked up at Handel again, and saw him as a worldly, practical man; I wondered if it was really because Italian opera had ceased making money that he turned his back on it and virtually created the oratorio as an alternative source of profit? Could so huge a change in so huge a man have been only the consequence of a fluctuation in income? Certainly, that would bring him down to size (always a pleasurable occupation among historians of a certain type. Caesar has feet of clay; I have feet of clay; therefore Caesar and I are a pair).

In 1727 there occurred an event that must have affected the course Handel was to take far more deeply than the presentation of *The Beggar's Opera* in the following year. In February 1727, Handel became a naturalized British subject. After some fifteen years' sojourn in this land, the cosmopolitan composer finally admitted to finding a home. England suited him, down to the pleasant, prosperous ground. He liked the language, he liked – even in that unequal age – the *sense* of equality and enterprise. Being a businessman, he liked the world of London where businessmen thrived and neither Church nor Court were able to dictate beyond their own narrow confines. He liked the plain, well-proportioned houses, the silver and glassware and the first-rate furniture of Chippendale and Sheraton and their followers. He liked the pleasure gardens of the capital – Vauxhall, Marylebone and Ranelagh – where he might sit and listen to his own music, played by a competent band. In short, he liked the life of a well-to-do Englishman. This act – of committing himself – could not but have affected him deeply. He had written English music before – many fine anthems, a 'Birthday Ode' and a 'Te Deum for the Peace of Utrecht'. He had assumed, with truly professional ease, the outward mantle of the only great English composer he knew: Henry Purcell; but nowhere, save in the masque, *Acis and Galatea*, had he really touched on Purcell's essential genius.

But now he had made his final decision (he was forty-two), and had sworn his allegiance, what could be more understandable for such a man – a man of the greatest honour – than that he should do more than just adopt the outward form of being English?

As always, with Handel, it was the heart he reached after, and the spirit. He found both in the literature, and particularly in the King James's Bible.

By far the greatest number of the oratorios are set either to Biblical words or to dramatizations of Biblical stories. In doing this he did not jettison his earlier love for opera; instead he translated it into an immeasurably richer state. The oratorios are operas on sublime subjects, where the action is in the music and all humanity is given a voice in the choruses. The presentation of *The Beggar's Opera* in 1728 merely accelerated a process that had already begun in Handel himself.

It was said of Henry Purcell that 'he was especially admired for the vocal, having a peculiar genius to express the Energy of English words . . .' He himself declared that: 'Music is the exaltation of poetry. Both of them may exist apart, but they are most excellent when they are joined.'

Handel began to set English words with an energy and understanding that all but surpasses his English predecessor. The great double chorus in 'Israel in Egypt' – 'I will sing unto the Lord' – is a most wonderful example of his setting a great English text. Listen to how the phrase, 'The horse and his rider', rears up in angular defiance, only to be submerged under the rapid, Red Sea waves of 'For He hath triumphed gloriously', while the grand statement of 'I will sing unto the Lord', wends its stately way through the turmoil, holding all the separate parts together as if in the mind of a watching host.

The text is taken directly from the 'Book of Exodus'; the music matches it in grandeur. It has often been remarked that Handel's music is at its finest in conjunction with great words.

In the year 1741, he wrote, in the space of twenty-four days, what has been called, 'the most remarkable work ever created by the human mind'. In April of the following year, 'Messiah' was given for the first time, in Dublin, and the proceeds were devoted to three charities for the relief of prisoners in debtors' gaols. Some 140 prisoners were released as a first consequence of 'Messiah'. Since then, many millions of human beings of all descriptions have been released from darkness by its transfiguring

10. George Frideric Handel

11. Sarah Siddons

12. Thomas Gainsborough

tenderness and optimism. To stand, as is the custom, when the Hallelujah chorus bursts out, is more than to follow the example of George II; it is to follow the heart which rises irresistibly to the music. Nor is it possible to be present at a performance of 'Messiah' without becoming a part of it, and without afterwards being mightily refreshed by that experience.

Before Handel left Dublin, he visited Dean Swift, whose choristers had taken part in the concerts. It is supposed that Handel went to thank him, and to renew an old friendship. But Swift was already mad and out of reason's and friendship's reach. Handel said nothing of their meeting; and maybe Dean Swift *knew* nothing of it.

'Messiah' was given in London in 1743, and, although not an immediate success, Handel was congratulated by a nobleman on having 'provided the Town with so fine an entertainment'. The compliment was not entirely to the composer's liking. 'I should be very sorry,' he said, 'if I only entertained them; I wished to make them better.'

In 1750 he presented this, his most highly valued work, even as Hogarth had done, to the Foundling Hospital. Yearly, until the end of his life, he conducted it in the Hospital Chapel; charity, especially charity towards children, was ever close to his heart. He died on Good Friday, 1759, and was buried, by his own request, in Westminster Abbey, leaving clear directions for 'any sum not exceeding six hundred pounds to be expended' for a monument to be erected there. He considered he had earned the honour but, like the man of integrity he was, wished to cover the expenses of it.

He was, in his younger years, a tall, big man, always well-dressed and generally considered fine-looking. To the end of his long life he spoke with a German accent, but his command of English was never in question. An Irish acquaintance, Dr Quinn, rated him a fine conversationalist (no small compliment from an Irishman), and said that:

> Handel, with his other excellences, was possessed of a good stock of humour, no man ever told a story with more. But it was a requisite

for the hearer to have a competent knowledge of at least four languages: English, French, Italian and German; for in his narrative he made use of them all.

He lived well and took pleasure in all the arts, possessing, among many well-made things, two paintings by Rembrandt, even though he himself doubted the authenticity of one of them. Although he never married, he enjoyed the company of women, and particularly the lively company of actresses. In his music, he put expression above technical facility, preferring an actress-singer, like Susanna Cibber with 'a mere thread of a voice' and the tenor, John Beard, who 'had but one note to his voice', to the marvellous but sexless warbling of the Italian eunuchs who had helped to make the opera ridiculous. His generosity extended beyond his public charity. Outliving, in the course of nature, friends and servants who were to have benefited under his will, he made provision instead for their dependants who were, quite possibly, unknown to him.

Occasionally it happens – perhaps once in a hundred years – that a human being expresses, not so much in his works as in his life, the genius of his age. In the days of Queen Elizabeth, it was Sir Walter Raleigh; in the days of the middle Georges, it was Dr Samuel Johnson.

The son of an unlucky bookseller in Lichfield, he rose, by his own industry, through layers of poverty and the ridicule attendant on the disfigurements of a skin disease and a melancholic nature, to become the most admired and venerated figure of his time.

Even as the age was one of extremes and contradictions – of filth and beauty, great indigence and great affluence, excessive delicacy and the foulest degradation existing, not so much side by side as together in one monstrous embrace – so Dr Johnson was a man of massive contrasts. Slovenly and unappetizing in attire, yet fastidious of mind; frequently brusque and sometimes brutal in conversation, yet capable of kindnesses that ennobled his age beyond its deserts:

His generous humanity to the miserable was almost beyond example. The following instance is well attested: Coming home late one night, he found a poor woman lying in the street, so much exhausted that she could not walk; he took her upon his back, and carried her to his house, where he discovered that she was one of those wretched females who had fallen into the lowest state of vice, poverty, and disease. Instead of harshly upbraiding her, he had her taken care of with all tenderness for a long time, at a considerable expense, till she was restored to health, and endeavoured to put her into a virtuous way of living.

When he was twenty-six, and miserably poor, he fell in love with and married a widow of nearly twice his age. Her fortune was scarcely larger than her lover's, who declared 'It was a love marriage on both sides'. Their progress to church was curious; Johnson himself relates it:

Sir, she had read the old romances, and got into her head the fantastical notion that a woman of spirit should use her lover like a dog. So, Sir, at first she told me that I rode too fast, and she could not keep up with me; then I lagged behind. I was not to be made the slave of caprice; and I resolved to begin as I meant to end. I therefore pushed on briskly, till I was fairly out of her sight. The road lay between two hedges, so I was sure she could not miss it; and I contrived that she should soon come up with me. When she did, I observed her to be in tears.

This lady was not handsome. David Garrick, the actor, described her as 'very fat, with a bosom of more than ordinary protuberance, with swelled cheeks, of a florid red, produced by thick painting, and increased by the liberal use of cordials; flaring and fantastick in her dress, and affected both in her speech and general behaviour.'

He loved her dearly, and, after her death, continued until his own to regard her as a paragon of the virtues and graces. It was said he had the use of only one eye. Truly, so far as Mrs Johnson was concerned, the great man resembled Voltaire's Memnon, the one-eyed porter who had not the eye that looked on the seamy side.

His chief literary work was his *Dictionary of the English Language*; besides this he wrote many poems, essays, *Lives of the Poets*, a stage tragedy called 'Irene', and a strange Abyssinian romance: *Rasselas*; this latter work composed rapidly, in a few days, in order to defray the cost of his mother's funeral. ('A man may write at any time, if he will set himself doggedly to it.')

He loved his country, yet had the good sense to declare that, 'Patriotism is the last refuge of a scoundrel.' He was a staunch Tory (ever loving old things), yet said, 'I would not give half a guinea to live under one form of government rather than another. It is of no moment to the happiness of an individual.'

In a warm mood, he said that: 'The applause of a single human being is of great consequence.' Yet he also said, to his most devoted admirer, 'Sir, you have but two topics, yourself and me. I am sick of both.'

He lived until his seventy-fifth year, a vast, shapeless grumble of a man, who sat his horse like a balloon and walked like a sack; and in his dread of dying, armoured himself with such a mass of superstitions that death, when it came, had to take him sleeping, else the battle would have been Titanic; and Johnson might have won.

The likeness of this giant was taken by a pygmy: a young Scottish lawyer, a man of more sex than sense and more vanity than either; a man extravagant in small things and mean in great ones, a silly, pushing man who perched on Dr Johnson much as certain birds perch on the rhinoceros and derive their food from the huge beast in return for relieving it of irritation (see plate 38).

Not that James Boswell spared his hero irritation; he pursued Johnson relentlessly, noting down his most insignificant remarks and provoking many an intemperate one. Never did an author worry an idea as Boswell worried Johnson; never did an author draw a man on the scale that Boswell drew Johnson.

Every man has a need to admire; the act of admiration enables us to accept our own faults with a good grace; it makes us feel we have a perception of higher things and are therefore relieved of the necessity of acquiring them. So James Boswell (whose nature would have fitted him to be a tax-collector, a publisher's

38. James Boswell

accountant or some other such mean thing), pursued his own grubby life and yet succeeded in raising a monument to the grandeur of mankind in *The Life of Samuel Johnson, LLD*.

Compared with Johnson's likeness in words, his likeness in paint would be laughable were it not sad that so much painterly skill should have been united with so little perception and understanding. Study the portrait how you will, nothing of a man emerges (see plate 39). How wretched that William Hogarth never painted Dr Johnson; how wretched that Sir Joshua Reynolds did.

39. Samuel Johnson

See! there he crouches – the artist himself; palette in one hand
and the other raised as if to shield his eyes from some intolerable
radiance, possibly inspiration. A fine painting, as a painting; an
emptiness as a man (see plate 40). Some men, of far less skill

40. Joshua Reynolds

than Sir Joshua, have the gift of immortalizing in paint; he only succeeded in embalming. He was, from all accounts, a charming and courteous man, eager to promote the interests of his fellow artists; but his efforts in that direction only produced a similar embalment: he founded the Royal Academy of Art. Perhaps he lacked, in the deepest sense, taste. William Hogarth, speaking to Horace Walpole, remarked that, 'Reynolds . . . t'other day offered a hundred pounds for a picture that I would not hang in my cellar.'

At the other end of the gallery, Hogarth on his shelf looks more pugnacious than ever as he almost glares towards his rival who was never his successor. Between them, along the walls, part linking them, part dividing them, hangs a gilded multitude of striking faces: Kitty Fisher (see plate 41), Sarah Siddons (see

41. Kitty Fisher

colour plate 11), several David Garricks . . . The stage, the people's art triumphant. Out of *The Beggar's Opera*, whose setting and characters demanded a new style of acting, came a most vigorous flowering of the theatre. Players, from being little more than posturing vagrants and the lowest of artists, leaped into the highest place of all, supplanting even those who created them. David Garrick, the greatest of them all, came to London from Lichfield in company with Dr Johnson who had been his master no less than his friend. Dr Johnson had twopence ha'penny in his pocket and the manuscript of his tragedy, *Irene*; David Garrick had three ha'pence and nothing else. But the actor prospered beyond the wildest dreams of the author, and it says much for Johnson's nobility of character that he was able to subdue his envy and praise Garrick, although not indiscriminately. He was wise enough to know that mankind is always more readily taken in by the appearance of a thing than the thing itself. It was Garrick's Hamlet, Lear and Macbeth that held the stage, rather than Shakespeare's.

Yet Shakespeare was Garrick's god; and almost single-handed he put the greatest Englishman of them all in a temple of which he was the high priest. The comedies of manners, the elegance of Restoration wit paled and shrank before the huge, resurrected figures of Lear, Macbeth and Richard III.

Hannah More, writing of Garrick's Hamlet, says:

> In every part he filled the whole soul of the spectator, and transcended the most finished idea of the poet. The requisites for Hamlet are not only various, but opposed. In him they are all united, and as it were concentrated. One thing I must particularly remark, that, whether in the simulation of madness, in the sinkings of despair, in the familiarity of friendship, in the whirlwind of passion, or in the meltings of tenderness, he never once forgot he was a prince; and in every variety of situation, and transition of feeling, you discovered the highest pitch of fine breeding and courtly manners.

('Transcended the most finished idea of the poet', 'the highest pitch of fine breeding'; the people's art seems to have undergone a small change.)

David Bate, writing in the *Morning Post*, on Garrick's Lear, remarks that:

> The curse at the close of the first act – his phrenetic appeal to heaven at the end of the second on Regan's ingratitude, were two such

enthusiastic scenes of human exertion, that they caused a kind of momentary petrefaction thro' the house, which he soon dissolved as universally into tears. – Even the unfeeling Regan and Goneril, forgetful of their characteristic cruelty, played thro' the whole of their parts with aching bosoms and streaming eyes. – In a word, we never saw before so exquisite a theatrical performance, or one so loudly and universally applauded.

'So exquisite a theatrical performance.' Although Shakespeare had been bidden into the drawing-room, like some vast uncouth labourer his breeches had been buttoned, and he'd been deprived of his tongue and boots. Even Hamlet was disallowed his duel, and the play's rough comedy dismissed. No one missed these things but the gallery, which grumbled audibly at the loss of its old friend, the gravedigger.

42. David Garrick

But who cared for the gallery, when, as Mrs More said:

> You will see half a dozen duchesses and countesses of a night, in the
> upper boxes: for the fear of not seeing him [Garrick] at all, has
> humbled those who used to go, not for the purpose of seeing, but of
> being seen, and they now courtesy to the ground for the worst places
> in the house.

When Garrick died, the friend he'd left far behind in worldly
success, wrote: 'I am disappointed by that stroke of death, which
has eclipsed the gaiety of nations and impoverished the public
stock of harmless pleasure.'

But it should be remembered that Dr Johnson also said that:
'To praise Garrick's Hamlet is to lampoon the age.'

Too well he sensed the fatal ease and certainty of the age, and
the unjustified confidence that was castrating it.

43. David Garrick

Every man was become his own Sir Isaac Newton and believed that the fall of a single apple had totally denuded the tree.

Reynolds' painting of Garrick is of just such an order: executed with the skill of a master, and with the eyes of a mole (see plate 42). Not that Sir Joshua lacked sensitivity. That's the extraordinary part about it. It's said he took three days to recover from the shock to his emotions after seeing Garrick as King Lear. But who would suspect it from the sleek, bland painting he did of the man?

There's a drawing, though, by George Dance, the architect, done barely three years after the painting by Reynolds, that really does capture something of the quicksilver man described by Dr Johnson to Mrs Thrale (see plate 43).

> 'David, madam,' said the doctor, 'looks much older than he is; for his face has had double the business of any other man's; it is never at rest; when he speaks one minute, he has quite a different countenance to what he assumes the next; I don't believe he kept the same look for half an hour together in the whole course of his life; and such an eternal, restless, fatiguing play of the muscles must certainly wear out a man's face before its real time.'

Beside where Sir Joshua Reynolds hangs, there is an archway in the gallery through which I caught a confused glimpse of scarlet uniforms and clashing steel; a phantasmagoria of savage generals and half blind admirals, and part of a legend: 'world power'. I shivered, and crossed the archway, coming to a halt almost with relief before that other luminary of English art, Thomas Gainsborough. Sensitive, but not intelligent-looking, he eschews the dramatic pose of his rival, and stands with becoming modesty beneath a tree. It is not, however, one of nature's trees; it is a Gainsborough (see colour plate 12). Although he seems to have been more partial to landscape than was Sir Joshua, he never succeeded in rendering it save as a background to a gentleman or a duchess. Even if they're not there, there is a distinct impression that they're expected and everything has been swept in readiness. If there was ever country mud in those days, Gainsborough never painted it; and his trees were great ladies in wood and leaves against whom it would have been treason for a dog to pee. Once, when asked for a view of real English scenery, he declined to oblige, fastidiously declaring that, 'With regard to real views from Nature in this country, I have never seen any place that affords a subject equal to the poorest imitation of Gaspar [Poussin] or Claude [Lorraine].'

Could art become more incestuous and absurd than that? To reject nature itself in preference to the inflated and improbable views of it expressed by other artists!

But here, hanging large above him is a fellow to set Gainsborough to rights! A countryman if ever there was one! See that weathered face, smiling ruddily at, doubtless, a good compost heap! A man close to the soil; a man whose word you'd take for the weather; a man who'd know a turnip from a duke and would sooner kneel to a cabbage than a king. Lancelot Brown, otherwise known as 'Capability Brown' on account of his habit of remarking on every vista that it was capable of improvement (see colour plate 13).

In this beaming gardener, the self-confidence of the age reached either its height or its depth, depending on the point of view. Deciding in his sturdy mind that nature abhorred a straight line, he created rolling hills and valleys where, unaccountably nature blundered and forgot its abhorrence of the flat. He made lakes where nature hadn't quite grasped the possibility of them; and he planted woods and copses where nature had been so unnatural as to omit them. Even as Gainsborough improved on nature in paint, so Capability Brown improved on it in itself. Someone once said that he hoped he would die before Mr Brown did, as he wanted to see Heaven before he improved it (see plates 44a and b).

The noble parks and estates that he laid out were bordered, not by walls or fences, but by sunken ditches, so that a gentleman's world should appear uninterrupted and that the prospect should appear limitless and eternal; nature without end. These sunken ditches were known as 'ha-ha's'. Why ha-ha? On the best authority, the expression is said to derive from 'Hah' – an expression of surprise. ('Hah! I didn't know there was a ditch here. You should have warned me –'.)

44a. Langley Park, Buckinghamshire. Garden laid out by 'Capability Brown'. Drawn by J. P. Neale and engraved by F. R. Hay.

44b. View of the Flower Garden at Nuneham Courtney, laid out by 'Capability Brown'. Engraving by Watts after Sandby.

45. Robert Adam

Beside Mr Brown sits Robert Adam, ineffably civilized and smiling up from a folio of engravings, for all the world like a bank manager contemplating the balance sheet of a successful century (see plate 45). Without a doubt, the finest English architect since Inigo Jones; a man of many ceilings and flawless proportions . . . to walk through an Adam doorway is to feel a gentleman. Compare his serenity of countenance with the troubled wonderment of his inspired predecessor, and gauge how far the world has come. Inigo Jones looks almost fearful of what the future holds. But one look at Robert Adam would have set his mind at rest; God's safely in His heaven, and Adam is in his garden of Brown.

His plaster decorations were a marvel of discretion and taste, and his fireplaces were of such surpassing elegance that, had they framed the eternal instead of the domestic fire, no gentleman would have shrunk from pulling up his chair – and roasting.

Half fascinated, half repelled, I glanced through the archway again, towards the inferno of flags and military colour, framed, as it were, by a giant Adam fireplace. Then I thought of Capability Brown's ha-ha's; I imagined them as part of a landscape in time. 'Hah!' cries out a generation, plunging haplessly down. 'You ought to have warned us there was a ditch!'

A little fat man, with big, round eyes, cautious brows and a sweet mouth that looks surprised to find itself above so many chins; a tubby soul who looks to have been reared on sugared plums and toffee, given as a reward for truthfulness and industry.

What a misleading face! Those big round eyes had looked, not on ways of pleasing, but most searchingly and unflinchingly into an abyss (see plate 46). This is Edward Gibbon, the historian, whose *Decline and Fall of the Roman Empire* charted the ruin of an earlier edifice that had seemed eternal.

Unlike his age which, since Newton, had looked for order in all things, and when it failed to find it, imposed an imaginary one that filled the bill, Gibbon set himself to describe things as they were and show that the catastrophic movement of history had been brought about by human beings and not the gods, or even God.

His immense work elicited yet another immortal remark from a member of the British Royal Family, a judgement that the first George – had he been fluent in the language – would have been

13. 'Capability Brown'

14. Horace Walpole

15. Fanny Burney

46. Edward Gibbon

proud to have uttered. Presented with the book (in some ways as significant a creation as any in the century), the Duke of Gloucester gazed at it and said: 'Another damned, thick, square book! Always scribble, scribble, scribble! Eh! Mr Gibbon?'

I sighed and looked again at Mr Gibbon, who, by an unlucky quirk of hanging, had been placed so that he must gaze for ever towards the madmen in the next room, preparing the way for yet another Decline.

In 1760 the second George had met his end by a stroke while straining in the privy (alas! without even a councillor to see him out). He was buried beside his beloved Caroline and the walls of their coffins were removed so that death should not separate them.

He was succeeded by his grandson, George III (see plate 47), who commenced his reign by meddling in politics and ended it hopelessly mad. A simple, good-hearted gentleman for whom the band played 'God Save the King' when he entered the sea to bathe, he was possessed of an ability, amounting to genius, for choosing bad advisers and replacing them with worse. And more than that, he took it upon himself to advise his advisers so that the smallest spark of sense they showed was instantly extinguished by their sovereign lord.

He was a family man; on a large scale. He saw himself as the father of his people, no matter where they were. He had the authority of John Locke, whose *Treatise on Government* established the throne (of William III) 'and made good his title in the consent of the people'. Power was morally vested in the king and his parliament by general consent, even as children yield to a parent and villagers to a squire.

Of all his children, those whom King George regarded with a peculiarly fatherly eye were the ones who'd set up house on the other side of the ocean: the American colonists. He did not seem to have shared Horace Walpole's view that:

> The next Augustan age will dawn on the other side of the Atlantic. There will, perhaps, be a Thucydides at Boston, a Xenophon at New York, and, in time, a Virgil at Mexico, and a Newton at Peru. At last, some curious traveller from Lima will visit England and give a description of the ruins of St Paul's, like the editions of Balbec and Palmyra.

He was not a literary man; he was a simple king and could not grasp the idea that his far-flung children in America did not see

47. George III

why they should pay taxes as long as they were unrepresented in parliament. To them, this was government without consent. They, too, had read John Locke, and had their own key to him.

(Truly, there were many keys to this complicated lock; and perhaps none of them has ever really fitted.)

So King George came the heavy father with the colonists, and they, in their turn, came the unruly children with him. As a final gesture, they flung a dish of tea in his face, and set about washing their hands of him – in blood.

Henceforth the old world was in decline, even as a great house from which the children have gone may sink into apathy while the woodworm burrows and the rafters rot.

The age that had begun with the Riot Act was ending in character. When the first George came to the throne there were some fifty crimes for which a man might have been hanged; by the end of the century there were something like three times that number. The common people, in the multiplying course of nature, were swarming now and it was necessary for men of property to erect defences against them. Why! when noble families left the town to season in the country, they were compelled to take even their doorknockers with them for fear of thieves. Nothing was sacred to the teeming rabble, so the hangman was kept busy expounding the ways of God to man. For they were vicious, these black-hearted newcomers from the shadows; they were also brutishly hungry. Starve a man's body, and he turns wild in his actions; starve a man's soul and he turns savage in his thoughts.

A mood of black depression momentarily came over me and, taking an advantage ironically denied the historian, I looked back along the gallery, while Edward Gibbon continued to stare incredulously the other way.

I supposed that the painting was screwed to the wall, else I'd have been tempted, in a mood of charity towards the dead, to have carried it to the opposite wall and let him face the other way. But even so, he'd still have been looking incredulous; the melancholy that crouched behind his eyes had arisen from a contemplation of the past, not the future.

Jonathan Swift was probably right; we really are 'the most pernicious race of odious little vermin that nature ever suffered to crawl upon the earth'.

It took scarcely half a minute to return to the bitter dean, clean across the century. For some reason or other I was surprised that the painting was still in its place. Not that anyone, ignorant of the sitter, would have wanted to steal it. It was a dreadful painting. One Charles Jervas, a pupil of Kneller, was responsible for it. Once, when he had finished a copy of a painting by Titian, he stepped back and said complacently, 'Poor little Tit! how he would stare!' The Age of Enlightenment it might have been; it was certainly not the age of self-enlightenment.

On Swift's grave is the inscription he himself desired to be put there: 'Where savage indignation can no longer lacerate the heart.' Well, well – Swift's in his coffin and all's hell with the world.

I thought Lady Mary Wortley Montagu was looking wistful. I almost spoke to her, then went on and the Kit-Kat Club raised their glasses as if in melancholy farewell. Nothing had changed Sir Robert Walpole, but I fancied even Handel looked suddenly despairing . . .

Another painting caught my eye, a pleasant portrait, smallish and in good taste. Previously it had been hidden from my view, for it was tucked in the annexe from which the attendant had appeared.

It is of a gentleman, not yet middle-aged. His lace-cuffed hand rests on a book, while behind him, out of a wooded landscape, rises the wing of a strange, fantastic mansion. I thought he was smiling at me, half encouragingly. A brittle, witty, marvellously intelligent face. Horace Walpole (see colour plate 14), unlikely son of the porcine Sir Robert. 'The world,' he said, 'is a comedy to those that think, a tragedy to those that feel.'

What was it to him? He smiles, as if to demonstrate his quality as a thinker. But to have written as he did, betrays that he also felt. Although the event that stirred him to the remark was the American Revolution of 1776, his dissatisfaction went deeper than that. The Age of Enlightenment was not proving altogether to his taste. While admitting a sane devotion to the purity of Classical Greece, he kept a corner in his heart for the dim, mysterious Gothic; the forgotten age of ancient castles, curses and,

above all, ghosts. The mansion behind him – Strawberry Hill –
is his Gothic fantasy made brick and stone. In it he wrote
The Castle of Otranto, a tale of supernatural terror in Italy, in a
remote and unhistorical past. This eminently cultured, shrewd
man rebelled in his inmost heart against the ordered clarity of
Locke and Newton, against the cataloguers who counted the
stars and made time-tables for the comets, and the systematizers
who threatened to dispel man's hopes and circumscribe his limitless imagination. He declared it as his aim to free the 'great
resources of fancy unfortunately dammed-up by common life'.

But Walpole, alas, was too clever a man to be taken in by
himself; he lacked that genius for self-deception that alone can
produce enduring works of art. His wonderful house and his
weird castle are really little more than the polite asides of a
gentleman, growing uncomfortable, but unwilling to trouble his
host.

> At present, nothing is talked of, nothing admired, but what I cannot
> help calling a very insipid and tedious performance; it is a kind of
> novel called *The Life and Opinions of Tristram Shandy*; the great
> humour of which consists in the whole narration always going
> backwards.

Thus Walpole on another rebel against the century's notions
of sanity and order. One rebel rarely likes another; each prefers
to swim against the tide alone; undiminished by company, and
followed, if must be, but not pursued.

Like Jonathan Swift before him, Laurence Sterne was an
Irishman who became an Anglican priest; only it was his wife
who went mad, not him. Her madness came on her while her
husband was writing *Tristram Shandy*. Now whether the novel
maddened her, or she maddened it, would take another Tristram
Shandy to determine; and, for my part, I'm not sorry to leave
the question in doubt.

The book is like a long, frantic conversation with a man who
won't let you get a word in edgeways, and who is so frightened
of silence that he must fill every natural pause with random

chatter for fear that a silence might provoke disquieting and terrible thoughts.

Again, like Swift, Sterne is filled with a spirit of criticism; but, so sad a way the century's gone, it is a criticism of art, not life. His humour and wit are devoted to a painstaking enquiry into what on earth he's doing, writing a story when it's plainly impossible to tell one.

The story begins nine months (exactly) before the birth of the hero, who does not appear until some four hundred pages later. After that he disappears again, but the talk goes on. It is a very long joke.

The author himself is set on a smallish pedestal, not very far from Swift. Unkindly, he's been done in marble, as if that was the only way of making him hold his tongue. Look at him – all nose, no chin and eyes blind with stony oddity. More than anything, he resembles a Roman emperor of the Saturnalia, king for a day of topsy-turveydom (see plate 48) . . .

It may well be that important works have flowed from *Tristram Shandy*, immense novels that dredge the muddy streams of human consciousness; but what is certain is that it is considered a very special thing to like *Tristram Shandy*. Men who dismiss *Gulliver's Travels* and *Robinson Crusoe* dote upon it. It has become a touchstone of taste, almost a secret society of art; an irritating giggle in a corner. You either like it or you don't. If you don't, then goodbye to you, sir! If you do, why then, welcome to Shandyism! A man who really likes *Tristram Shandy* is a man who – really likes *Tristram Shandy*! Thus the world is divided. There are, of course, other ways of dividing the world, but on reflection, it would seem more desirable to unite it. And this *Tristram Shandy* will never do. It lacks the capacity to inspire love.

What, then, will inspire love? What is the necessary ingredient? Love itself, perhaps? What then is love?

> In our last book we have been obliged to deal pretty much with the passion of love; and in our succeeding book shall be forced to handle the subject still more largely . . . that what is commonly called love

48. Laurence Sterne

namely, the desire of satisfying a voracious appetite with a certain
quantity of delicate white human flesh, is by no means that passion
for which I here contend. This is indeed more properly hunger; and

as no glutton is ashamed to apply the word love to his appetite, and to say he LOVES such and such dishes; so may the lover of this kind, with equal propriety, say, he HUNGERS after such and such women.

Thus Henry Fielding, a man made almost on the same scale as Dr Johnson, Handel and Hogarth. A man of overflowing humanity; a great magistrate of wisdom and compassion, and a man who believed, with all his heart, in the saving grace of laughter. Not Reynolds nor Gainsborough were the successors to Hogarth, but Henry Fielding, even as he was the successor to Daniel Defoe and the author of *Don Quixote*. *Tom Jones* comes roaring out of the century with a vitality no inferno could diminish. It is, as he called it himself, a comic epic in prose; and never was the Classical stream (for wantonly Classical it is) sailed to a more hilarious advantage.

Here is the venerable Homer, at full stretch in the *Iliad*:

> It was now that Telemonian Aias struck down Athemoin's son, Simoisius. This sturdy youngster took his name from the river Simois, beside which he was born when his mother was returning from Mount Ida, where her father and mother had taken her to see their sheep. His life was too short for him to repay his parents for their loving care, for it ended when he met the great Aias' spear. He had scarcely sallied out when Aias struck him in the breast by the right nipple. The bronze spear went clean through his shoulder and he came down in the dust, felled like a slender poplar with a bushy top that has shot up in the big meadows by a stream and is cut down by a wainwright with his gleaming axe. Later, the man will make felloes from it for the wheels of a beautiful chariot; but he leaves it now to lie and season on the bank. Thus King Aias felled Simoisius, Athemoin's son.

Whew! And here is Henry Fielding at full stretch, in *Tom Jones*:

> Recount, O Muse, the names of those who fell on this fatal day. First, Jemmy Tweedle felt on his hinder head the direful bone. Him the pleasant banks of sweetly winding Stour had nourished, where he first learnt the vocal art, with which, wandering up and down at

wakes and fairs, he cheered the rural nymphs and swains, when upon the green they interweaved the sprightly dance; while he himself stood fiddling and jumping to his own music. How little now avails his fiddle! He thumps the verdant floor with his carcase. Next, old Echepole, the sow-gelder, received a blow on his forehead from our Amazonian heroine, and immediately fell to the ground. He was a swinging fat fellow, and fell with almost as much noise as a house. His tobacco-box dropped at the same time from his pocket, which Molly took up as lawful spoils. Then Kate of the Mill tumbled unfortunately over a tomb-stone, which catching hold of her ungartered stocking inverted the order of nature, and gave her heels the superiority to her head. Betty Pipkin, with young Roger, her lover, fell both to the ground; where oh perverse fate! she salutes the earth, and he the sky. Tom Freckle, the smith's son, was the next victim to her rage. He was an ingenious workman, and made excellent pattens; nay, the very patten with which he was knocked down was his own workmanship. Had he been at that time singing psalms in the church, he would have avoided a broken head. Miss Crow, the daughter of a farmer; John Giddish, himself a farmer; Nan Slouch, Esther Codling, Will Spryy, Tom Bennet; the three Misses Potter, whose father keeps the sign of the Red Lion; Betty Chambermaid, Jack Ostler, and many others of inferior note, lay rolling among the graves.

And so it goes on: uproarious parody, uproarious love-making, uproarious satire on pedantry, hypocrisy and all the follies that try to keep a good heart from its lawful prey. In the end, Tom Jones, that many-adventured foundling, weds his Sophia and, 'Mr Jones appears to be the happiest of all humankind; for what happiness this world affords equal to the possession of Sophia, I sincerely own I have never yet discovered.'

A feeling of optimism began to return; an optimism that no quantity of Shandy could have inspired. I looked about me for a portrait of the magnificent Mr Fielding; but alas, he never had his likeness taken. Only a drawing by his friend Hogarth, done from memory some years after his death, remains. Not only were Fielding and Hogarth great friends, but in their work they complemented each other. What Hogarth did for the town, Fielding did for the countryside. But, even as the countryside is gentler than the town, Fielding is necessarily gentler than Hogarth. A landscape with a tree in it is a more suitable subject for pleasantry than one with a gallows.

Fielding's last novel, *Amelia*, was much affected by his work as a magistrate, for which he was paid yearly 'three hundred pounds of the dirtiest money in the world'. Social problems loom large in *Amelia*, and the comedy is much subdued; even so, there was someone who wrote:

> You will guess that I have read *Amelia*. Indeed, I have read but the first volume. I had intended to go through with it; but I found the characters and situations so wretchedly low and dirty, that I imagined I could not be interested for any one of them.

Who wrote that? A rival – that's plain. No one but a rival could adopt so angry and high-minded a tone to something as harmless as a novel. What manner of rival? A pompous, narrow-minded old woman of a man? Possibly. A man of no talent himself? Ah! that's another matter. Talent and good sense have never been renowned for going hand in hand. Although there's a distinct borderline between genius and madness, there's none at all between genius and sheer stupidity.

The man was undoubtedly an ass; and, to prove it, there he stands, not far from Horace Walpole, whose smile grows weary and contemptuous. Everything about the man proclaims him to be pompous and small-minded, from the fat hand cuddling the ample stomach to the neat, freshly laundered wig framing the prudish face (see plate 49). Yet this man's work outsold Fielding, Swift, and probably the Bible itself. Even Dr Johnson was moved to say that: 'There is more knowledge of the heart in one letter of Richardson's, than in all *Tom Jones*.'

Samuel Richardson, son of a joiner; a well-to-do printer of little formal education, but able to write agreeable letters. In 1740, two booksellers suggested to this printer that it might be a profitable thing to employ his skill and compile a polite letter-writer for the benefit of uneducated people unable to compose

49. Samuel Richardson

THE HOUSE OF HANOVER

their own. It was further suggested that the letters should refer to everyday situations, such as might be met with in the ordinary course of life, so that the purchaser might be able to copy them out with little or no alteration. The situation that at once presented itself to Richardson's mind was a local event he'd heard of, and plainly thought long about. A servant girl in a great house had so successfully resisted her master's amorous attentions that eventually he'd been driven to marry her.

Richardson set about composing a series of letters between just such a servant girl and her parents. He became fascinated by the whole thing in the most extraordinary way; the letters got quite out of hand. The respectable printer pursued the subject with quite unwholesome zeal and eventually burst out of the letters into a daily journal of the hectic events as one Mr B. repeatedly attempted the virtue of Pamela, his pretty maidservant, at every conceivable time and in every conceivable place. The terrified fluctuations of Pamela's mind are faithfully recorded for the benefit of her awed parents as their distressed daughter struggles to maintain her purity of both body and soul. The odds against Pamela are enormous; she is abducted, held prisoner, the world seems set on her ruin; but, although her shameless master's hand becomes tolerably familiar with her bosom, he never reaches her heart until the tribulations of some eight hundred pages have brought him to a declaration of marriage.

This protracted seduction, this marathon progress to the marriage bed, succeeded as no piece of fiction had ever succeeded before. It became an opera, a play, a household decoration, and an object of clerical approval, of uniting, as it did, the pleasures of sex with the sanctity of wedlock. The virtuous Pamela, forever removing herself from the grasp of the tormented Mr B. struck the deepest chords in the unlikeliest hearts. Duchesses dreamed of being Pamela; while Pamelas dreamed, with renewed hope, of being duchesses.

It has been said that Richardson was not quite so artless as he seemed; that his Pamela was, perhaps, calculating in her virtue; that her frequent confidings to her parents of how pretty everyone thinks her, suggest the sharp little hypocrite who has invested

her heart in her looks and meanly waits for the interest to accumu-
late. But if that were so, it would make out Richardson to be as
great an ironist as Henry Fielding; and that he never was. He was
most bitterly offended when the possibility of hypocrisy in his
beloved Pamela was unkindly put by Fielding in *Shamela*; he
was cut to the quick when his romance itself was ridiculed by the
same author in *Joseph Andrews*, a despicable tale of Pamela's
footman brother whose impeccable virtue is assailed by a lady.

Outraged, Richardson sought to crush Fielding forever under
the huge weight of *Clarissa Harlowe*, the longest novel in the
language. Fielding, uncrushed, replied with his own epic, *Tom
Jones*, and Richardson, incensed to the point of apoplexy, retali-
ated with *Sir Charles Grandison*, to show Henry Fielding and the
world how a real country gentleman behaved.

This rivalry of letters had, at least, a more prosperous outcome
than that which had earlier killed off the Italian opera; both the
comic epic and the novel of sentiment seemed to gain strength by
rebounding from each other; but, although Fielding was the
greater genius and immeasurably the greater man, Richardson's
success and influence were undoubtedly more widespread.

Lady Mary Wortley Montagu disdainfully declared that
Pamela would delight all the chambermaids in Europe. It did;
and their mistresses too. Not since the apple had been offered to
Eve in the Garden of Eden had such a stimulus been given to the
imagination of women. On one level, Richardson's achievement
was outstanding; he had shown how it was possible to represent
the thoughts and feelings of a human being in the framework of a
narrative so closely detailed as to be wholly credible. On another
level, his achievement was even more striking. By presenting a
woman as being conscious of both a man's sexuality and her own,
and by suggesting that hers was under better control, he elevated
women to a degree of civilization and sensitivity utterly denied
them in the easy-going world of *Tom Jones* and the bawdy plays
of Wycherley and Vanbrugh. He made sex itself, rather than
passing fornication, the subject of a novel; and at a stroke he
captured the huge audience of women who, until then, had been

invited to banquets of art in which they were represented merely as the dishes rather than the meat and wine.

This much he accomplished, not by rebelling against any established order, or by seeking originality, but by bringing into the world of art and culture a degree of naturalness and reality that provided a common ground of experience for cottage and mansion to share in. The novel; that extraordinary amalgam of ancient romance, poem and play; that greatest child of the century that was able to embrace the world and move the silent reader by the fire – with nothing more than a printed page – to laughter, tears, and a wiser understanding of himself and his neighbour next door.

I saw pretty Fanny Burney, sharply pensive under her enormous hat (see colour plate 15). Honourable lady; she it was who first seized on Richardson's brilliant notion and composed her own novels in letters: *Evelina* and *Camilla* . . . Jane Austen admired her tremendously. What was it Miss Austen said about such works?

> . . . only some work in which the greatest powers of the mind are displayed, in which the most thorough knowledge of human nature, the happiest delineations of its varieties, the liveliest effusions of wit and humour are conveyed to the world in the best chosen language.

'It's stopped raining, sir,' said the attendant, coming upon me unawares.

With surprise I discovered myself to be at the foot of the stairs, standing blindly before the drawing of Jane Austen, by her sister (see plate 50). I had passed clean through the bloody inferno of 'world power', without even noticing it. I thought Miss Austen would have approved; she didn't have much time for it herself. Although she admired sailors, she was no lover of battles.

The attendant nodded at the portrait and then smiled at me.

'If it was just for pleasure given, sir,' he said; 'then she'd be right at the top.'

'And why not?'

50. Jane Austen

'If you'll forgive my reminding you, sir, that wasn't your
opinion earlier.'
'That was a hundred years ago.'

'So now it's all just to please?'

'It's no little thing.'

'What of Mr Handel wanting to make people better? What of Hogarth and Dean Swift?'

I shrugged my shoulders. 'You don't make people better by *dis*pleasing them.'

'Nor just by pleasing them, either, sir.'

'Does it matter in the end?'

'I'd be sorry, sir, if that was the only feeling you brought out of the House of Hanover with you. I'd be sorry if you forgot Dr Johnson's carrying the sick woman home, or Dr Swift writing about Stella, or Mr and Mrs Hogarth caring for foundlings in their own home, or Handel giving "Messiah" to charity, or a thousand and one other acts of generosity and mortal goodness.'

'But they are facts, deeds . . . they are not works of art.'

'Do you not think so, sir? Is art only what's written down?'

'What else?'

'I always understood that art – the best art, that is – draws its substance from life, while the art that comes of itself alone is a dead thing – even though some folk can make a habit of it. The best art is really second-hand, you might say; as good a copy as can be made of a feeling worth passing on.'

'You make it sound even less than a simple means of pleasure.'

'Not when it preserves something as important as a fine action, a warm heart or a generous love.'

'In fact, or in fiction?'

'All fact is fiction, sir, once it's passed out of sight.'

'And history – this great gallery of the dead?'

'Fiction, sir, to do with what you will. Go through the gallery again – and come out with a different answer. Go through it backwards, even, and watch men dwindle; see the kings turn back into gods and all the rest of mankind shrink into the shadows. Fiction, sir; it's all in the mind. Every last one of them, from Daniel Defoe to Samuel Richardson, goes out into the street with you –'

'How lucky,' I said, fumbling for the medallion that represented my umbrella, 'how lucky that it's not raining.'

꠵꠵꠵꠵꠵

TIME CHART

꠵꠵꠵꠵꠵

	Political	Social	Cultural
1714	Accession of George I. The Riot Act		
1715	The Jacobite Rebellion		John Gay's *Trivia* published
1716			Death of Wycherley
1717	Triple Alliance: France, Great Britain and the United Provinces		'Water Music' party
1719			*Robinson Crusoe* published
1720		The Mississippi Company in France and the South Sea Company in England both collapse. Huge numbers ruined. Farenheit invents thermometer	
1721		Riots of weavers	
1722	Rise of Sir Robert Walpole	Death of Duke of Marlborough	
1723			Death of Sir Christopher Wren
1726		Mutiny of convicts	Death of Vanbrugh *Gulliver's Travels* published
1727	Death of George I. Accession of his son, George II and Queen Caroline	Death of Isaac Newton	

	Political	Social	Cultural
1728			*The Beggar's Opera*
1729			Death of William Congreve
1731		Publication of Jethro Tull's *Horse-hoeing and Husbandry*, a work of great agricultural importance	Death of Defoe
1733	War of Polish Accession. Violent opposition to Walpole's Excise Bill	John Kay invents the flying shuttle, which will double the output of weavers	
1735		Abraham Darby succeeds in smelting iron from coke	Hogarth's 'The Rake's Progress' published
1736		Gin riots in London	
1737	Death of Queen Caroline		Tom Paine, author of *Rights of Man*, born
1738		John Wesley's first Methodist Association	
1739	War with Spain (War of Jenkin's Ear)		Handel's *Saul* and *Israel in Egypt*
1740			Richardson's *Pamela* published
1742	Fall of Sir Robert Walpole		Handel's 'Messiah' Fielding's *Joseph Andrews* published
1744	War with France Accession of Louis XVI		
1745	Jacobite Rebellion		Death of Swift
1749	Peace with France	Steel smelted in England	Fielding's *Tom Jones*
1751	Death of Frederick, Prince of Wales (Father of George III)		
1753			British Museum founded
1756	Seven Years' War Black Hole of Calcutta		
1757	Pitt–Newcastle Ministry Clive's Victory at Plassey		

	Political	Social	Cultural
1759	Fall of Quebec to General Wolfe	Halley's Comet (predicted in 1704)	Death of Handel Voltaire's *Candide*
1760	Death of George II Accession of George III Fall of Montreal	Bakewell experiments with selective breeding of cattle in England	
1761	George III marries Charlotte of Mecklenburg-Strelitz		
1762		Rousseau's *Contrat Social*	
1763	Peace with France in Canada	Wilke's Riots	
1764		Hargreave's Spinning Jenny	Mozart (aged 8) composes his first symphony in London and is examined by the Royal Society
1766	Repeal of American Stamp Act		
1767		John Hunter experiments with venereal diseases	
1768		Cook's voyage to Australia	Royal Academy founded
1769			Royal Crescent in Bath built by John Wood
1770	Lord North becomes Chief Minister of George III		
1772		Food riots in London	
1773	Boston Tea Party		
1774		Priestly discovers oxygen (dephlogisticated air)	
1775	American War of Independence		
1776	Declaration of Independence	Invention of steam engine by Watt	
1778	France joins America in war against England Death of Pitt the elder	The City of London protests about the war being a 'discredit on humanity'	
1780		Gordon Riots in London	

	Political	Social	Cultural
1781		Further protests by City against American war	
1782	Fall of Lord North		J. C. Bach (son of J. S. Bach) dies in London
1783	End of American War Pitt the Younger Prime Minister		
1784			Death of Doctor Johnson
1785		Cartwright invents the power loom	Mozart's *Marriage of Figaro* produced in Vienna
1787		First convicts sent to Botany Bay	
1788	George III's first attack of madness; attempts to throttle the Prince of Wales who, however, is disappointed in his hopes of accession as his father recovers		*The Times* first published
1789	Fall of the Bastille and beginning of the French Revolution		
1790			Burkes' *Reflections* on the French Revolution
1791			Tom Paine's *The Rights of Man* Haydn's first visit to London
1792	Paine elected to French convention as member for Calais Attempt to burn down the House of Commons		
1793	Execution of Louis XVI War with Revolutionary France	Financial distress in the City of London; many bankruptcies	
1794	Reign of Terror in France Lord Howe's victory over French fleet	Five pound notes first printed by Bank of England	Haydn's second visit to London

	Political	Social	Cultural
1796	Rise of Napoleon	Vaccination against smallpox discovered by Jenner	
1797	Battle of Cape St Vincent	Spithead Mutiny Death of John Wilkes Marriage of John Adams (afterwards President of U.S.) in Barking	
1798	Battle of the Nile		
1800		Shortage of bread in London; bakers prohibited from selling loaves less than 24 hours out of the oven	Royal College of Surgeons incorporated

🐍🐍🐍🐍🐍🐍

BIBLIOGRAPHY

🐍🐍🐍🐍🐍🐍

SOURCE MATERIAL

Addison, Joseph and Steele, Sir Richard. The *Spectator*. Everyman Library, Dent, London

Antal, Frederick. *Hogarth and His Place in European Art*. Routledge, London, 1962

Ed. Ford, Boris. *Pelican Guide to English Literature Vol. 4. From Dryden to Johnson* and *Vol. 5. From Blake to Byron*. Penguin, Harmondsworth, 1970

Boswell, James. *Life of Johnson*. Everyman paperback, Dent, London, 1973

Burney, Charles. Ed. Mercer, Frank. *General History of Music*. Dover, London, 1935

Burney, Fanny. Ed. Gibbs, Lewis. *Diary*. Everyman paperback, Dent, London, 1972

Clark, Sir George. *Later Stuarts 1661-1714. Oxford History of England Vol. 10*. Oxford University Press, Oxford, 1962

Dean, Winton. *Handel's Dramatic Oratorios and Masques*. Oxford University Press, Oxford, 1959

Defoe, Daniel. *Robinson Crusoe*. Everyman paperback, Dent, London

Defoe, Daniel. *Moll Flanders*. Everyman paperback, Dent, London

Fielding, Henry. *Tom Jones*. Everyman paperback, Dent, London, 1963

Fielding, Henry. *Joseph Andrews* and *Shamela*. Everyman's University Library paperback, Dent, London, 1972

Flower, Newman. *George Frideric Handel*. Cassell, London, 1959. Panther, London, 1972

Gibbon, Edward. *Decline and Fall of the Roman Empire*. Everyman Library, Dent, London, 1960

Halsband, Robert. *Life of Lady Mary Wortley Montague*. Oxford University Press, Oxford

Hogarth, William. Ed. Burke, Joseph and Caldwell, C. *Hogarth, the Complete Engravings*. Thames and Hudson, London, 1968

Homer. Trans. Rieu, E. V. *The Iliad*. Penguin, Harmondsworth, 1970

Lang, Paul Henry. *George Frideric Handel. Reappraisal of his Life and Works.* Faber, London, 1967

Mitchell, R. J. and Leys, M. D. R. *History of the English People.* Pan Books, London, 1967

Plumb, John Harold. *Death of the Past.* Macmillan, London, 1969. Penguin, Harmondsworth, 1973

Sterne, Laurence. *Tristram Shandy.* Penguin, Harmondsworth, 1970

Summerson, John. *Georgian London.* Barrie and Jenkins, London

Swift, Jonathan. Ed. Doren, Carl Van. *Portable Swift.* Chatto, London, 1968

Swift, Jonathan. *Gulliver's Travels.* Everyman paperback, Dent, London, 1961

Swift, Jonathan. *Battle of the Books and Other Satires* (includes The Tale of a Tub). Everyman paperback, Dent, London, 1969

Watson, J. S. *Reign of George III 1760–1815. Oxford History of England Vol. 12.* Oxford University Press, Oxford, 1960

Watt, Ian. *Rise of the Novel.* Chatto, London, 1957. Penguin, Harmondsworth, 1972

Willey, Basil. *Eighteenth Century Background.* Chatto, London, 1946

Williams, Basil. *Whig Supremacy, 1714–1760. Oxford History of England Vol. 11.* Oxford University Press, Oxford, 1962

Other titles that are out of print
but which may be obtainable from public libraries

Ed. Abrahams, G. *Handel, a Symposium.* Oxford University Press, Oxford

Ed. Agate, J. *English Dramatic Critics.* Barker, London

Besant, A. *London in the Eighteenth Century*

Harrison. *English Lawyer.* Edn. 1838

Holland, A. K. *Henry Purcell.* Penguin, Harmondsworth

Phillips, H. *Mid-Georgian London.* Collins, London

Walpole, H. Ed. Lucas. *Letters.* Newnes, London

FICTION

Aiken, Joan. *Black Hearts in Battersea.* Cape, London, 1965

Aiken, Joan. *The Whispering Mountain.* Penguin, Puffin Books, Harmondsworth, 1970

Aiken, Joan. *The Wolves of Willoughby Chase.* Cape, London, 1962. Penguin, Puffin Books, Harmondsworth, 1971

Bacon, Martha. *Sophia Scrooby Preserved.* Gollancz, London, 1971

Boston, Lucy M. *Children of Green Knowe.* Faber, London, 1954

Boston, Lucy M. *Chimneys of Green Knowe.* Faber, London, 1964

Bourliaguet, Leonce. *Guns of Valmy.* Abelard-Schuman, Aylesbury, 1968

Burton, Hester. *Castor's Away.* Oxford University Press, Oxford, 1962

Burton, Hester. *Time of Trial.* Oxford University Press, Oxford, 1963

Burton, Hester. *Otmoor For Ever*. Hamish Hamilton, Antelope Books, London, 1968

Dickens, Charles. *Barnaby Rudge*. Penguin, Harmondsworth, 1973

Dickens, Charles. *A Tale of Two Cities*. Bancroft, London, 1967

Falkner, J. Meade. *Moonfleet*, Penguin, Puffin Books, Harmondsworth, 1970

Garfield, Leon. *Jack Holborn*. Longman, Young Books, London, 1967. Penguin, Puffin Books, Harmondsworth, 1970

Garfield, Leon. *Devil-in-the-Fog*. Longman, Young Books, London, 1966. Penguin, Puffin Books, Harmondsworth, 1970

Garfield, Leon. *Smith*. Longman, Young Books, London, 1967. Penguin, Puffin Books, Harmondsworth, 1970

Grice, Frederick. *Aidan and the Strollers*. Penguin, Puffin Books, Harmondsworth, 1964

Heyer, Georgette. *The Masqueraders*. Heinemann, London, 1952

Heyer, Georgette. *These Old Shades*. Heinemann, London, 1952. Pan Books, London, 1972

Manning, Rosemary. *Boney Was a Warrior*. Hamish Hamilton, Antelope Books, London, 1966

McGregor, Iona. *Edinburgh Reel*. Faber, London, 1968

McGregor, Iona. *Tree of Liberty*. Faber, London, 1972

Neill, Robert. *Hangman's Cliff*. Cedric Chivers, Portway Reprint, Bath, 1969

O'Brian, Patrick. *Golden Ocean*. Macmillan, London, 1970. Penguin, Peacock Books, Harmondsworth, 1972

Orczy, Baroness. *The Scarlet Pimpernel*. Brockhampton, Knight Books, London, 1970

Ed. Politzer, Anie and Michel. *My Journals and Sketchbooks: Robinson Crusoe*. André Deutsch, London, 1974

Scott, Sir Walter. *Heart of Midlothian*. Everyman paperback, Dent, London

Stephens, Peter John. *Shadow Over Welesmere Gap*. André Deutsch, London, 1971

🐚🐚🐚🐚🐚

Works from the National Portrait Gallery
reproduced in this book

🐚🐚🐚🐚🐚🐚

Richard II	Artist unknown
Henry V	Artist unknown
Henry VIII	after Hans Holbein
Thomas Cranmer	Artist unknown
Jane Seymour	photogravure after Holbein
Anne Boleyn	Artist unknown
Katharine Parr	attributed to W. Scrots
Sir Philip Sidney	Artist unknown
Robert Dudley, Earl of Essex	Artist unknown
Sir Walter Raleigh	attributed to monogrammist H(?Hubbard)
James I	Daniel Mytens
Ben Jonson	after A. Blyenberch
John Donne	after I. Oliver
Inigo Jones	after Vandyke
Charles I	Daniel Mytens
Samuel Pepys	John Hayls
John Bunyan	T. Sadler
John Locke	John Greenhill
Henry Purcell	J. Closterman
John Dryden	Godfrey Kneller
Daniel Defoe	Artist unknown
Joseph Addison	after Godfrey Kneller
Richard Steele	Godfrey Kneller
Third Earl of Burlington	after Godfrey Kneller
Alexander Pope	W. Hoare
Lady Montagu	Artist unknown
Jonathan Swift	C. Jervas
George I	from the studio of Godfrey Kneller

Two noble members of the Kit-Kat Club	Godfrey Kneller
Sir Robert Walpole	Jean Baptiste Van Loo
George Frideric Handel	Thomas Hudson
John Milton	Artist unknown
James Boswell	Joshua Reynolds
Samuel Johnson	Joshua Reynolds
Joshua Reynolds	self-portrait
Kitty Fisher	N. Hone
David Garrick	Joshua Reynolds
David Garrick	drawing by George Dance
Robert Adam	Artist unknown
Edward Gibbon	Henry Walton
George III	from the studio of Alan Ramsay
Laurence Sterne	marble bust by J. Nollekens
Samuel Richardson	J. Highmore
Jane Austen	drawing by her sister
Elizabeth I	Artist unknown
Shakespeare	Artist unknown
Charles II	E. Hawker
Sir Christopher Wren	Godfrey Kneller
Queen Caroline	J. Amigoni
Sarah Siddons	G. Stuart
Thomas Gainsborough	self-portrait
'Capability Brown'	N. Dance
Horace Walpole	J. G. Eccandt
Fanny Burney	Edward Frances Burney

INDEX